YOU'RE RICHER THAN YOU THINK

Erwin W. Lutzer

While this book is designed for the reader's
personal enjoyment and profit, it is also intended for group study. A leader's guide is
available from your local Christian bookstore
or from the publisher at $2.25.

VICTOR BOOKS

a division of SP Publications, Inc., Wheaton, Illinois

Offices also in Fullerton, California • Whitby, Ontario, Canada • London, England

Recommended Dewey Decimal Classification: 234
  Suggested Subject Headings: Salvation; Redemption

Library of Congress Catalog Card Number: 78-056619
ISBN: 0-88207-777-5

© 1978 SP Publications, Inc. World rights reserved
Printed in the United States of America

VICTOR BOOKS
A division of SP Publications, Inc.
P. O. Box 1825 ● Wheaton, Illinois 60187

Contents

Foreword 6

1 Becoming What You Are 7

2 You Are Part of an Eternal Plan: Election 13

3 You Are Declared Righteous: Justification 25

4 You Live in the Presence of God: Access 37

5 You Have a New Family: Sonship 47

6 You Have Spiritual Power: The Holy Spirit 59

7 You Are a Precious Possession: God's Inheritance 69

8 You Serve a New Master: Identification with Christ 79

9 You Are Victorious Over Satan: Authority 89

10 You Are Free From the Law: Grace 99

11 You Have Citizenship in Heaven: Glorification 109

12 How Then Should We Live? 119

To my sisters
Ruth and Esther
whose missionary service has always
been an inspiration to me.

Foreword

Some books you read because you need the message. Others you read because the author is unique and has a gift for saying old things in new ways, things that are important to your success in living.

This book you read for both reasons.

The message is important. Most Christians do not really understand what happened to them when they trusted Christ. They have a vague understanding of the great words of the Gospel, like justification, grace, election, and the like—but they don't quite understand what those words can mean in their daily Christian walk. This book tells you.

And the author is unique. Erwin Lutzer is the rare combination of scholar, preacher, and pastor. Head and heart work together in this man's life, and both are dedicated fully to Jesus Christ. He is beloved by students in the classroom, appreciated by believers in the pews, and greatly admired by those of us who are fortunate enough to be among his friends. He makes us think, and he helps us go deeper with Christ.

So, in your hands you have an important book written by a unique man. I predict that his ability to state profound truths in simple words, and then beautifully illustrate them from daily life, will utterly captivate you. I have enjoyed reading every book Erwin Lutzer has written, and I have been helped by them.

This book is no exception.

Warren W. Wiersbe

1

Becoming What You Are

Would you exchange places with the angel Gabriel? Think carefully before you answer. On the spur of the moment you might be tempted to say, "Of course!"

But I wouldn't. Not because my career can match his—indeed I can't even imagine what it must be like to be a swift, powerful creature who runs errands for the Almighty. Nor is it because I have the gifts Gabriel does—angels have scores of abilities that we can't even comprehend. Gabriel has many advantages over us mortals: freedom from sin, swift interplanetary travel, special privileges as God's messenger, and power to combat evil forces. Added to this is the honor shared with other angels, of worshiping in the presence of the living God.

Striking as these advantages are, angels never experience God's grace like we do. God elevates us to a status that angels might be tempted to envy—we are heirs of

God and joint-heirs with Jesus Christ. Because we are accepted in the Beloved One, God loves us as He loves His Son; He accepts us with the same finality and satisfaction. Angels cannot claim that distinction.

In Psalm 8, David compares angels and mankind. Part of this psalm is quoted in the Book of Hebrews. The *New American Standard Bible* translates the Hebrew passage as, "Thou hast made Him for a little while lower than the angels; thou hast crowned Him with glory and honor, and hast appointed Him over the works of Thy hands" (Heb. 2:7). Notice the phrase "for a little while." The implication is that man is lower than the angels, but this is only temporary. Because of God's grace, we have privileges that the angels cannot enjoy.

Many people believe that the Christian life is a self-improvement program. We are challenged to be active, dedicated and committed. Otherwise, we are made to feel guilty, worthless and like second-class citizens of the kingdom of heaven. Some pastors exhort Christians to upgrade their spiritual lives, by wrongly appealing to their willpower and their obligation to serve God.

This does not bring lasting results. Sometimes we can temporarily change by our own efforts. Indeed, we can choose to become involved, more consistent in church attendance and can even break sinful habits by sheer determination. But something is missing. We can do all these things and remain completely unchanged on the inside.

Once we see ourselves as God sees us, we can stop living the Christian life by sheer will power. Let me put it this way: when we accept Christ as Saviour, God immediately gives us special recognition, status, authority, power and a host of privileges. If we are ignorant of these, we will dutifully plod through life quite certain that Christianity isn't all that it is supposed to be. We will be powerless to achieve spiritual victory when sin rears its ugly head, and there will be no love, joy and peace through the hardships of life.

Evangelist Peter Dyneka left his homeland as a teenager on March 11, 1898. He sailed from Libau, Russia, bound for Halifax, Nova Scotia, on the SS *Dvinsk,* a Russian liner. For 14 days and nights the sturdy Russian ship pushed its way through the stormy Atlantic. Peter's mother had packed enough food for him for the whole voyage. The box was so large that an older friend carried it on board ship for him.

Every day he longingly looked through the window of the door leading into the ship's dining room and envied the wealthy people who were able to eat in luxury. Peter walked past them to his room to eat his black bread and garlic.

Later, some of the sailors tricked Peter into helping them with their chores. "If you help us work in the kitchen, we will give you meals in return," the wily sailors promised. Dutifully, Peter worked for the rest of his meals across the Atlantic.

It wasn't until the last day of the voyage that he learned that three daily meals in the ship's dining room were included in the price of the ticket!

Many of us know that our tickets to heaven are free, but we don't understand the privileges which are included. Some of us will discover (perhaps near the end of our lives) that the very blessings we sought so earnestly were already included with the gift of salvation. God is generous. He loves to give, and He wants us to receive. Paul wrote, "He who did not spare His own Son, but delivered Him up for us all, how will He not also with Him freely give us all things?" (Rom. 8:32, NASB) It's the "all things" that this book explores.

Improving Your Self-Image

Ever give a four-year-old boy a cowboy hat? He'll ride every article of furniture. The carpet becomes a pasture and every imaginable object becomes a cow. It's a basic axiom of psychology that we become what we perceive ourselves to be.

A plastic surgeon performed an operation on a girl who had a hooked nose. She was shy and withdrawn, convinced that no one could love someone as ugly as she. After the surgery, the doctor carefully removed the bandages and was extraordinarily pleased with his work. The girl looked beautiful. But when he held the mirror so that she could see herself, she remarked, "I look no different!" The doctor was astounded, for it was obvious that the operation had been a triumphant success. This girl had thought of herself as being ugly for so long that she could not accept what she was now. Several months later she began to believe that she was different—maybe even beautiful. Her personality began to change; she became cheerful and friendly. Now she saw herself as an attractive person, one who could be a success, and she acted accordingly.

Similarly, it is not easy to accept all that we are in Jesus Christ. Many of us balk at the idea that God sees us as perfect in Christ. We struggle with accepting the special attention God gives us as His children. We are convinced that these lofty advantages can't really be ours.

But they are. Bit by bit, we must believe what God has said and stop living by our haphazard feelings and hunches. As we focus on what we are and what we have in Christ, the veil of unbelief will fall away. Then we can begin the process of being changed into Christ's image by His Spirit. But first we must find out who we are in Christ.

Living By Praise

As we grasp God's generosity toward us, we spend more time praising God than asking Him for special blessings. A deeply committed Christian man lived a defeated life. He prayed for victory over discouragement and worry but nothing helped. He decided to go off by himself to "pray through" until he experienced victory. Even this was unsatisfying. Somehow God seemed so far away and victory was as elusive as ever.

Then in prayer, he realized that he had been living in unbelief. He had been asking God for blessings which had accompanied his salvation. Like Peter Dyneka, he had been conned into working for a menu that was already paid for.

So he began to praise God, habitually and consistently. Like the girl who had plastic surgery, he came to realize what he was in Christ. The result? He discovered that God is as good as His Word. He could live like God intended. He was freed from slavery to sin. But it took the Holy Spirit's illumination for him to see that these benefits were included when he accepted Christ.

Little wonder that Paul's prayer for the church at Ephesus was that "the eyes of your heart may be enlightened, so that you may know what is the hope of His calling, what are the riches of the glory of His inheritance in the saints, and what is the surpassing greatness of His power toward us who believe" (Eph. 1:18-19, NASB).

Only the Holy Spirit, through the Word of God, can give us insight into the privileged relationship we can enjoy with Jesus Christ. The need of the moment is for understanding, enlightenment, appreciation and praise.

Ethel Waters, who died at the age of 80, became well known in Christian circles because of her singing at numerous Billy Graham crusades. She was the product of a rape relationship—a 14-year-old girl was raped, and Ethel was born. About her background she said, "A child growing up needs laps to cuddle up in. That never happened to me. Never. It's a real tragic hurt, wantin' to be wanted so bad."

Yet after she committed herself fully to Christ, she said, "I keep praising the Lord so much I don't have any other hobbies!" You can be sure His eye was on that sparrow.

In Christ we can move out of our past into a meaningful present and a breathtaking future. Not that life's struggles will become easier, but the end results will be satisfying. We will grow and appreciate God's grace toward us more. "Therefore if any man is in Christ, he is a new creature; the old things passed away; behold new things have come" (2 Cor. 5:17, NASB).

As a believer in Jesus Christ, you can draw on supernatural sources. At your disposal are the necessary ingredients for a satisfying life: the attention, love and generosity of Almighty God are at this moment, yours.

This book explores your inheritance. You shall discover that *you're richer than you think.*

2

You Are Part of an Eternal Plan: Election

You've seen a building under construction: boards, bricks and steel girders are stacked around the freshly dug excavation site. Day after day the work crew pieces the materials together. Gradually, the unconnected haphazard materials emerge into a new building.

How does such a transformation take place? By following a detailed blueprint. An architect, or perhaps several of them, spends countless hours drawing plans which include everything from the apex of the roof to electrical outlets.

If we as humans are intelligent enough to know that a building cannot be constructed without a master plan —if we know that every window and brick must be chosen to fit the blueprint—obviously God would not have created us without a specific plan in mind. He has infinite wisdom, that means that we were designed for a specific purpose.

The Bible teaches that long before we were born, God had already prepared for our arrival on this earth. Most Christians admit that God has a plan for them, but they don't understand how that can be relevant to them *now.* "What good is God's plan for my life if He doesn't show it to me?" we've all been tempted to ask.

Fortunately, in the Bible, the curtain of mystery that divides the human race from God is pushed back and we are invited to peek into the plans and aspirations of Almighty God. There we find that we are not an afterthought. Rather, our life on earth is part of a drama that God planned ages ago.

Think carefully about this verse from the Book of Ephesians. Speaking of God, it says, "Just as He chose us in Him before the foundation of the world, that we should be holy and blameless before Him" (1:4, NASB). Perhaps you as a believer in Jesus Christ thought that *you* chose Christ to be your Saviour. I'm sure you did, but this verse teaches that God chose you before you chose Him.

Already I can hear a chorus of objections to the idea that God actually selected certain people to belong to Him and therefore by-passed others. "That isn't fair. We're just robots and this leads to fatalism." But keep reading. We can't ignore the doctrine of election because it is puzzling or even because we might object to its implications.

Who Made the Choice?
This doctrine is so difficult to accept that many Christians assume that God did not do the choosing at all. Rather, they believe we chose God and because He knew beforehand how we would choose, He chose us on that basis. In other words, God chose us because He foreknew we would choose Him.

Visualize it like this: before the foundation of the world, God knew who would accept His Son and who would not. On that basis He then called some His "elect." This explanation is based on passages of Scripture such as Romans 8:29, "For whom He foreknew, He also predestined to be conformed to the image of His Son, that He might be the firstborn among many brethren" (NASB). Then in 1 Peter 1:1-2 we read that believers are "chosen according to the foreknowledge of God the Father" (NASB).

This view of election stresses that although God foreknows that certain people will believe on Christ, He does not *cause* them to do it. In other words, God does not interfere with our freedom. We can choose as we wish. God does not initiate the choice. If we are among the elect, it is because of our choice, not God's.

Now if you accept this interpretation of election, you are in good company. Many Christians find it satisfying. The problem, however, is that the Bible teaches that God did the choosing and we choose Him because He chose us first.

We are elect "according to foreknowledge," but that word *foreknowledge* means more than simply "knowing ahead of time." By checking other passages, we conclude that *foreknowledge* means "to regard with favor." For example, Amos quotes God as saying to Israel, "You only have I known of all the families of the earth" (3:2).

Similarly, the New Testament uses the word *foreknowledge* in the sense of "foreloved." Paul wrote in Romans, "God has not rejected His people whom He foreknew" (11:2, NASB). Again, foreknowledge cannot merely mean "to know in advance," rather it refers to God's special favor. Other passages support this understanding of the word (Matt. 7:23; 2 Tim. 2:19; 1 Peter

1:20). To be elect according to foreknowledge, is to be chosen on the basis of God's special favor. Such passages cannot prove that God chose us simply because He knew ahead of time that we would believe.

Sometimes verses such as 2 Peter 3:9 which teach that God desires that all men be saved, are used to prove God did not do the choosing. But look at it this way: of course, God is compassionate and, therefore, does not desire that people be lost. But the simple fact is that He has chosen not to fulfill all of His desires. For example, He does not desire to see people suffer, yet He chose not to intervene when Hitler inflicted incredible torture on millions of people. God did not desire this; furthermore, He had the power to stop it, but He didn't. In the same way, God does not delight in the death of the wicked, yet for reasons unknown to us, He has not prevented their eternal retribution. Even if one does not accept the doctrine of election, it is obvious that God could prevent the eternal suffering of hell: Satan could be destroyed, we could be born without a sin nature and hence be more inclined to choose God, and sinners such as Judas could have died at birth (Jesus said it would have been better for him if he had not been born). At any rate, God has chosen not to follow all of His desires, perhaps because His other attributes limit His choices.

Is God Unfair?

You're asking: On what basis did God select the ones He did—was His choice arbitrary? Is God unfair? What about those who aren't chosen? A seminary professor once appropriately said, "Try to explain election and you may lose your mind. But try to explain it away and you may lose your soul!" Yet since the Bible speaks about election we cannot ignore it, even though it involves deep mystery. Let me answer these questions as best I can.

First, we do not know the basis upon which God chose His people. That remains an inscrutable mystery which God has not revealed. But we do know that the choice was *not* arbitrary.

Sometimes people think that God selected a certain number of people at random, almost like a lottery. But all of His decisions are consistent with His attributes of love and wisdom. The choosing was not done haphazardly. When God chose His people, He could do so because for Him there are no surprises. Not only did He choose certain individuals to be saved, He also planned the *context* in which they would be converted. That's why I have never wondered whether my children are among the "elect." Why? Because I know that if a child is faithfully taught the Word of God, his usual response will be to accept Christ as Saviour. Remember, God not only plans who will be saved but also *how* they will be saved. That explains why there are so many Christians who grew up in Christian homes. It also explains why we ought to witness. God accomplishes His purposes *through us*.

In other words, God's decision to save us involved planning where we would be born, how and when we would hear about Jesus Christ and even the circumstances that would lead us to accept Christ as Saviour. Election is only a part of the total picture.

What about God's justice? Could a righteous God select some and not others? Remember, that none of us deserves to be saved. If God saves anyone, it is because of His mercy, not because He owes us salvation. If I see ten children in an orphanage and choose one of them to be mine, can the others charge me with injustice? No, because I owed none of them a home. I need not have chosen any; my selection was due to mercy. Similarly, Paul taught that election displayed God's grace (Rom. 11:5).

Someone protests, "You couldn't adopt all those children, but God is omnipotent. He could have chosen *all* to be saved." Perhaps. But since we do not know all of God's purposes, we must be cautious in saying what God can or cannot do. At any rate, we cannot charge Him with injustice.

We should not conclude that God causes people to sin. He is not the immediate cause of evil choice; we do evil because we are sinners. James taught that if we succumb to temptation, we cannot blame God (James 1:13-15). Hence God holds us responsible for our actions.

Yet in the discussion of the doctrine of election, Paul knew that God's justice would be questioned. People will argue that God cannot hold men responsible if they are not chosen. In Romans he anticipates this objection. He expects an objector to ask, "Why does He [God] still find fault? For who resists His will?" Paul's reply: "On the contrary who are you, O man, who answers back to God? The thing molded will not say to the molder, 'Why did you make me like this,' will it?" (Rom. 9:19-20, NASB)

Paul's point is that such questions are out of order. The creature has no right to judge the Creator. If God wishes to display His glory by exercising His sovereign power, we are in no position to judge Him. That's tough to accept, but that is Paul's reply. We must remain silent, and not judge God.

And what about the non-elect? Perhaps you are not a believer in Jesus Christ. You're wondering: How can I know whether or not I am among God's chosen people? Maybe you're tempted to become fatalistic. If God does the choosing, "whatever will be, will be!"

Wait a moment. Before you go on, you can find out whether you are a member of the elect. Here's how: Pray to Jesus Christ, admitting that you are a sinner and ask Him to accept you on the basis of His death on the cross (this is more clearly explained in the next chapter). If you do this, Christ has promised to receive you and hence you can know you are included in His special plan (John 6:37). Your response to Christ is proof that the Holy Spirit is already working in your life to draw you to the living God (John 6:65).

Someone explained it this way. Visualize a doorway with the words, "Whosoever Will May Come," inscribed above. We invite people to enter the door and after they have entered, they turn around and above the inside of the door they see the words, "Chosen From Before the Foundation of the World."

When people accept Christ they don't realize that this was arranged from the beginning. Someday, we will see that salvation begins with God and ends with Him. It is the work of the triune God. The Father planned redemption and chose those who would be saved; the Son died so it could be accomplished; then the Holy Spirit gives us the ability to believe and accept it. Salvation is of the Lord.

A missionary taught the doctrine of election to a small group of believers in South America. He did so with hesitation, knowing that the doctrine is difficult to understand. The next day one of the believers told the missionary, "After what you told us about election, I couldn't sleep all night!" The missionary was apprehensive, thinking that he had raised too many questions in the man's mind. But the new believer continued, "I couldn't sleep because I was so overwhelmed with the thought that God would actually choose *me!*"

That should be our response. Though we cannot answer all the problems raised by the doctrine, and though we are tempted to question God, our response should be one of humility and thanksgiving. We should never lose the wonder of God's sovereign purpose in our behalf.

God's Choice

When did God choose us? *Before* the foundation of the world. Scientists disagree in their estimates regarding the age of the earth. It could be several billion years old, or it could be more recent. But before God created the universe, *He already had you in mind.*

That's staggering. Philosophers tell us that God does not exist in time but in an eternal "now." That might be true, but it's difficult for us to comprehend because we exist within a time sequence. And in some way, God chose us before time had its beginning. In fact, since God is eternal, we have always been included in His plan.

Back when there was nothing—nothing except God —He planned the creation of the earth, the existence of angels, the whole drama of redemption and *you* were known to Him by name. A crucial question today is: Who am I? People of all ages are known to drop out of society "to find themselves." If you are a believer in Jesus Christ, you are a special individual chosen by the Almighty to be His child. You are *not* an afterthought. Even if you were born into a family that did not want you, you are an important member of a divine family that does. God chose you before the sun shone and the earth began its incessant rotation.

What was God's purpose in choosing us? Let's look at Ephesians 1:4 again, "Just as He chose us in Him before the foundation of the world, that we should be holy and blameless before Him" (NASB). Perhaps you are struggling with God's will for you. Maybe you are wondering whether to change your vocation or perhaps you are trapped in a cruel marriage relationship. If you are a believer, God has a plan for you that can be accomplished *right where you are.* It is that you be holy and without blame before Him. But who wants to be holy?

Today we have a distorted idea of what the word *holy* means. We think holiness is hypocritical, or maintaining an aura of piety. But the word holy means "wholeness." It means that we fulfill the purpose for which we were created. Physically we are whole when our bodies function as they are intended to; spiritually we are whole when we are in fellowship with God. Holiness is not drudgery or following a boring routine. It is being all that we were created to be.

God also desires that we be *blameless.* Again many of us are uncomfortable with this word. We have all made wrong decisions; we've sinned deliberately. But the word *blameless* is not the same as the word *sinless.* We can be sinful and still be blameless. The sacrifice of Christ on the cross is the reason why we can be blameless before God, even though we are sinners.

What About Me?

Perhaps all of this is new to you. You're overwhelmed by God's incomprehensible plan. How can you apply this to your life? What difference should it make in your attitude? In your home? You'll want to digest these implications.

First, God's will is not primarily a matter of geography or vocation. Even if you have made foolish choices in the past, that doesn't mean that God is through with you. He chose you to be holy and blameless before Him in love, and that is possible regardless of where you are or the entanglements you have experienced. In other words, God is more concerned about what you *are,* than what you *do.*

Second, you as a believer exist only for the glory of God. Read this carefully, "Worthy art Thou, our Lord and our God, to receive glory and honor and power; for Thou didst create all things, and because of Thy will they existed and were created" (Rev. 4:11, NASB) ·

What is the purpose of life? To earn a decent living, save money for an enjoyable retirement and then die? No. You were created by God and for His pleasure.

He planned your life beforehand, even your physical features were formed under His supervision, "For Thou didst form my inward parts; Thou didst weave me in my mother's womb. I will give thanks to Thee, for I am fearfully and wonderfully made; wonderful are Thy works, and my soul knows it very well" (Ps. 139:13-14, NASB).

But what about those born with physical handicaps —is God responsible for this condition? He says *yes.* "And the Lord said to him, Who has made man's mouth? Or who makes him dumb or deaf, or seeing or blind? Is it not I, the Lord?" (Ex. 4:11, NASB) We exist for God, and life becomes easier when we accept His authority.

Third, your death, as much as your life, is a part of God's eternal plan. We read that Christ's enemies could not take Him because "His hour was not yet come" (John 7:30). His appointed time to die had not yet arrived. Of course, Christ's life and death are far more important than ours, but His was minutely planned in the same way as ours. God takes note of the sparrow that falls to the ground; indeed the very hairs of your head are numbered. And for you, as for Christ,

" . . . we know that God causes all things to work together for good to those who love God, to those who are called according to His purpose" (Rom. 8:28, NASB). If you submit to God's will, everything, including the time of your death, is under God's supervision. Someone has said, "If you are to be hung, you'll never drown!" God is never caught off guard by the unexpected.

Finally, God's eternal plan helps you discover your personal identity. You are not a card in a giant computer. Jesus, speaking of Himself as the Good Shepherd, says, "When He puts forth all His own, He goes before them, and the sheep follow Him because they know His voice" (John 10:4, NASB).

Christ knows who you are, though you might be filled with doubts, fears, anxieties and crushed dreams. Or perhaps you are riding high on a wave of excitement or the elation of a personal victory. Either way, Christ knows you and loves you.

The good shepherd crosses every bridge ahead of you. Missionaries who leave for a strange and distant country can be assured that God is the best booking agent. He never sends you anywhere without making plans for your arrival. Remember, there are no emergencies in heaven.

Rejoice! You are a part of God's eternal plan, "Chosen in Christ before the foundation of the world."

3

You Are Declared
Righteous: Justification

"But I've blown it so badly!" the young man protested when I suggested that his ugly past could be forgiven. "I don't want to come to God until I can *prove* that I mean business!"

His story? He grew up in a Christian home and went through the motions of accepting Christ as his Saviour at the age of eight. But for some reason it never "took." He dropped out of church before he reached his teens and began to associate with the wrong group of friends. He got hooked on pornography and occasionally tried drugs. Before he was 20 he had fathered a child, married and divorced (in that order). Now he wondered how God could accept him.

His question was the same that we all ask when we finally admit we need divine help: how can I become worthy of God—what can I do so that He will accept me?

This young man had tried to meet God—at least he prayed occasionally, sometimes desperately. Once he even had a "religious" experience, a vague feeling that maybe God could accept him, forgive him. But he wasn't sure. The experience vanished, his prayers went unanswered and he was left confused, thinking that some day in the future he would prove himself. He wasn't about to trouble God until he was worthy of God's attention.

This concept reflects that of countless people throughout the centuries. The monks of the Middle Ages tried to shut out the world and find God in their own souls. Others fasted or abused their bodies to demonstrate their desire for God's pity and attention. Yet for all this, many admitted they still felt guilty, spiritually restless and unsure whether they had won God's approval. What has gone wrong? Why are some people not sure they have found God, even though they seek Him with diligence?

Medieval Justification

Suprisingly, the difficulty can be traced to a misunderstanding of the New Testament doctrine of justification by faith. Without realizing it, many of us think of God as the medievals did: He accepts only those who become worthy of His forgiveness by proving their sincerity and yieldedness. As a minimum, they believe that God's acceptance fluctuates with their actions.

In medieval times *justification* was interpreted to mean that God *makes* people righteous. The church taught that we must become righteous before God will accept us. Of course, it was believed that we cannot make ourselves righteous, but we could become righteous with divine help. People were taught that God infuses grace into a believer, thus aiding the long, torturous process of becoming holy. If a person displayed an unusual amount of grace—if it appeared that he had achieved a high standard of righteousness—he became a *saint.* Thus the doctrine of the canonization of saints arose.

Unfortunately, there were only a few who qualified for such high honors. Most of the common people realized that they had little chance of achieving such an excellent record. They knew that their lives fell far short of what a perfect God would require. How could they gain God's favor? In order to give people hope, a new doctrine was needed.

To enhance the possibility that sinners could be accepted by God, the doctrine of purgatory was invented. Purgatory was supposed to be an intermediate place where souls were purified to meet God's standards. People were encouraged because even though they had not become saints, they had a chance to enter heaven eventually (hopefully).

Faced with such doctrines, most of the people chose one of two life-styles. Either they dedicated their lives to attain holiness with God's help and thus opted for the monasteries, fasts and monotonous prayers; or they lived recklessly, certain that holiness was impossible. The vast majority gave up before they began.

Now whether the young man who sat across from me realized it or not, he was back in the Middle Ages theologically. He wanted to convince God that he meant business. He even thought that if he suffered sufficiently for his sin (primarily the emotional trauma of guilt) that God would then accept him and forgive his sins. That's why he didn't want to come to God until he knew he could "hold out." He thought that God would accept him only on the condition that he (the young man) would demonstrate his sincerity, desperation and fortitude. Only then would he be worthy of God's approval.

Against such an understanding of justification, Martin Luther staked his life. He saw clearly that if God insists that we become worthy of His acceptance—then two results follow. First, we can never have any assurance of heaven, for not even the most exalted saint possesses the perfection God requires. *If we must become perfect to enter heaven, no one is going there!*

Second, Luther saw that such a view led to mental and emotional slavery. No one knows how high God's standard is; hence we cannot be satisfied that we have met His requirements. Are 50 lashes to the body sufficient to curb the desires of the flesh—would that be enough to please the Most High? If not, what about 51? Peace of mind becomes impossible. There can only be uncertainty, doubt and guilt.

To return to the young man referred to earlier: can he ever be sure that he will be able to hold out? If he thinks he must pay for his sin through guilt feelings, how much mental suffering does God require? How and when can he *know* that he has finally merited God's grace? He cannot. Despair will become a way of life.

New Testament Justification

Martin Luther's study of the Book of Romans led him to an answer to this dilemma. Luther knew that God could not compromise His attribute of righteousness to accept sinners. That was intolerable and impossible. He also saw clearly that no man could claim he had become righteous enough to enter heaven. How is the impass bridged?

From his study of the Book of Romans, he concluded that justification meant that God *declared* us righteous, even though we still remain imperfect, unworthy and sinful. Read Paul's quotation of an Old Testament passage regarding Abraham, "For what does the Scripture say? 'And Abraham believed God, and it was reckoned to him as righteousness' " (Rom. 4:3, NASB). That word *reckoned* is a legal term, often used when crediting money to someone's account. More specifically, Paul writes, "But to the one who does not work, but believes in Him who justifies the ungodly, his faith is reckoned as righteousness"(Rom. 4:5, NASB). Other uses of the word *justification* prove that it refers to God's declaration that we have been *credited* with the righteousness of Christ (Gal. 3:8, 11).

God's pronouncement that we are righteous is made *outside* of us. It is not an act that we experience within our lives. Now, of course, there are many things that we do experience in the Christian life—the gift of the Holy Spirit, for instance. But justification is a *legal* pronouncement made independently of any personal experience. In fact, God's declaration that we are righteous doesn't *in itself* change our character.

Many years ago a man was driving through Europe in a Rolls Royce. The car had mechanical difficulties, and two mechanics flew from England to the continent to repair the engine. The owner of the car expected to receive a bill from the factory, and when none arrived, inquired about the cost of the repair job. The reply he received from the factory read something like this, "We have no record of two mechanics flying to Europe to repair your car. In fact, we have no record of any mechanical difficulty ever occurring in a Rolls Royce."

We are imperfect, in desperate need of repair, but God has no record of our shortcomings. Even in the Old Testament He assured His people, "I have wiped out your transgressions like a thick cloud" (Isa. 44:22,

NASB). Our sins are blotted out so completely that He does not remember them. He never holds them against us again.

Surprisingly, having Jesus Christ in our hearts does not qualify us to enter heaven. The reason is simple: Even with Christ in our hearts we are not perfect. But we must be perfect to enter heaven. How can we then be sure of God's acceptance? When we trust Christ as our Saviour, all of His moral perfections are credited to our account; we are considered as perfect as Christ. God's act of justification is the legal basis for our entrance into heaven.

God could not give us this gift of righteousness if Jesus Christ had not become the propitiation for the sins of all mankind (Rom. 3:25). That word *propitiation* means mercy seat. In Old Testament times the priest would meet God in the Holy of Holies on one day of the year (Yom Kippur) to sprinkle blood on the mercy seat. There God and man met together. Similarly, it is Christ's death that makes possible our reconciliation to God.

A man in California pleaded guilty to a traffic violation. The judge announced that the defendant would have to pay a fine for the misdemeanor. But the moment the judge demanded the fine, he left the bench, walked down and stood next to the defendant and paid the fine for him! The judge handed down the sentence, but he also paid it.

So it is with God. He has cataloged a list of our sins in Romans 3:9-18. No one is qualified to correct the shattered relationship between God and man. Man's hope of becoming righteous enough for God to accept him fades into oblivion. Paul pictures a huge courtroom in which the whole world appears before God. No one has met the stringent demands of God's law.

"Now we know that whatever the law says, it speaks to those who are under the law, that every mouth may be closed, and all the world may become accountable to God" (Rom. 3:19, NASB).

A gruesome spectacle. The offense is so great that only God can straighten it out. He delivers the guilty verdict. Then He identifies Himself with the human race; He becomes one of us, dies on a cross and satisfies His own just requirements. Those who accept His sacrifice for their sins are acquitted. Their sins are forgiven, they are declared perfect.

Augustine expressed it this way, "O Lord, demand what You will, but supply what You demand!" God demands perfection from His creatures, but if they will ever have it, He Himself must supply it. We need not be concerned about how high God's standard is, as long as He meets it for us.

Thus the sacrifice of Christ guarantees our acceptance before God. We don't have to wait until we are living differently before we are reconciled to God. God doesn't accept us because of our promise to "hold out," or because we've demonstrated our sincerity, or have suffered for our own sins. No, the basis is the completed work of Jesus Christ.

The Way to Freedom

Many Christians are confused at this point. They think, "I've had such a profitable time in my devotions today —surely God will accept me now." Or conversely, if they have yielded to sin, they think, "I can't ask God's forgiveness until I've suffered a while so that He knows I really am sorry." They are constantly looking within their own bankrupt souls for some good reason why God ought to accept them. Understandably, they are troubled with guilt and doubt God's forgiveness. The reason? They are trying to establish a relationship with God on a wrong basis.

Suppose you were about to board a plane at an airport. Would it be necessary for you to demonstrate your sincerity before being allowed to enter the plane? Would it matter whether you felt worthy to fly, or could prove that you could "hold out" all the way? No, only the ticket counts. Similarly, our acceptance is based only on Christ. He alone is the ticket. *Nothing* else matters.

John White in his book *The Fight* describes the vicious circle we have all experienced: "For many years I grappled with the problem of how I could live a holy life. I attended spiritual life conferences of different kinds in different countries and received conflicting counsels and various degrees of temporary help. I read every book I could get my hands on about 'victorious living.' Often I would feel I had turned a major corner in my life and would seem finally to be in possession of the secret of sanctification. But I could no more hang on to the secret than capture a sunbeam in my pocket."[1]

And how was he set free from the emptiness of his Christian experience? Read his words carefully, "Light began to break over me when I realized in the depths of my spirit that I was forgiven, cleansed, accepted, justified *because of what Christ had done for me* and not because of the depth of my yieldedness."[2]

Once we understand the implications of justification, we need not wait until the right moment to return to God, every moment is equal, for the basis of our relationship with God is unchangeable. That basis is unrelated to our performance; it resides in Christ.

---

[1] John White, *The Fight: A Practical Handbook to Christian Living* (Downers Grove, Illinois: InterVarsity Press, 1976), p. 184.

[2] *Ibid.*, p. 186.

Remember that justification means that God wipes out all of our sins, past, present and future. When you transfer your trust to Christ alone, you are declared righteous from that moment until the day you die and enter God's presence. Notice what Paul wrote, "And when you were dead in your transgressions and the uncircumcision of your flesh, He made you alive together with Him, having forgiven us all our transgressions, having cancelled out the certificate of debt consisting of decrees against us and which was hostile to us; and He has taken it out of the way, having nailed it to the cross" (Col. 2:13-14, NASB). Christ met *all* the demands of the law for us.

If this is so, then why are we asked to confess our sins? "If we confess our sins, He is faithful and righteous to forgive us our sins and to cleanse us from all unrighteousness" (1 John 1:9, NASB). Confession is necessary for fellowship. Sin builds a barrier between us and God. We feel guilty, the Holy Spirit is grieved and our ability to rely on God's power diminishes.

Confession, which means to agree with God regarding our sin, restores our fellowship. It is a form of discipline which God requires. But our sin does not affect our *legal* standing. Even when our sin is unconfessed, we still are God's children and have Christ's righteousness credited to us.

An illustration might help. The prodigal son remained a son even when he was far from home. He had all the legal rights of sonship and permanent acceptance by his father. But he did not enjoy these benefits until he returned home and admitted, "Father, I have sinned" (Luke 15:11-32).

When we understand the basis of our acceptance we can return to the Father quickly, and confidently. Sorrow for our sin, yes. Guilt for confessed sin, no.

The Basis for Christian Experience

God accepts all believers *equally;* there are no degrees of acceptance. D. L. Moody, John Wesley, and Hudson Taylor did not have a special quality of righteousness attributed to them. God only accepts the absolute righteousness which Christ provides. This is credited to all believers without discrimination, qualification or prejudice. Believers all share the same privileges. There are no special favors reserved for the superstars of Christianity. We are all on the same level in the presence of the living God.

Now that we are declared righteous, God is legally free to bless us. He can bestow special privileges upon us, since our acceptance before God is as secure as Christ's; God's love can now be freely exercised toward us. "He who did not spare His own Son, but delivered Him up for us all, how will He not also with Him freely give us all things?" (Rom. 8:32, NASB)

Have you ever wondered how a holy God can elevate sinners to the position of being "heirs of God and fellow-heirs with Christ"? (Rom. 8:17, NASB) God makes no distinction between us and Christ so far as righteousness is concerned. That's why we can be married to Christ as His bride, and also why Christ is not ashamed to call us His brothers (Heb. 2:11).

All the blessings we have in Christ are ours because we are accepted in Him. Believers have *already* been blessed with all spiritual blessings in heavenly places in Christ. We need not seek a "second blessing." God does not withhold something from some believers until they "pray through" or fulfill a certain spiritual standard. Of course, we must yield, surrender and sometimes agonize before God in prayer, but the reason is *not* to receive from Him a blessing He is reluctant to give us. Rather, our yielding prepares our hearts to receive the blessings which are already legally ours in Christ.

That's why we never get beyond the doctrine of justification. It's the foundation that supports all of the other benefits we receive from Christ.

Yes, that young man can be forgiven—even though he hasn't proven himself or is unsure whether he can "hold out." He must understand that the basis for God's acceptance is not his ability or promises, but Christ's finished work.

4

You Live in the
Presence of God: Access

You have been granted an appointment with the President of the United States. You're excited; apprehensive. You've rehearsed your protocol, determined to make a good showing. Moments later you step onto the plush carpet of the oval office. Your mind goes blank; you forget your lines—you just stand and stare. . . .

That's how one man described his experience when he was invited to chat with the President. The trappings of power and fame can be spellbinding. When you are there, you are awed by it.

If you could spend one hour with any person in the world, who would it be? The President? A movie star? A famous athlete? Chances are you'd snatch the opportunity (I know I would) and you'd rearrange your schedule to make time for the appointment.

What if you could talk to God for 10 minutes—really talk to Him—would you do it?

Does this make you uneasy? Somehow talking to God is different from talking to the President or some other national celebrity. You can *see* them, but God is invisible. In fact, sometimes He seems far away and impersonal.

Then there is an added problem: would He take notice of you or me? Christianity teaches that God is an infinite and perfect Spirit who encompasses the whole universe. He's got so much to control, so much to supervise. Would He really want me to make an appointment with Him?

The answer is yes. In fact, He is seeking for worshipers . . . admirers if you please, people whose hearts are drawn irresistibly to Him (John 4:24). The reason that you were created was to spend your life worshiping, loving and glorifying God.

Tuning In to God

If you are a believer, Christ has already brought you into the presence of the Almighty. Whether you are aware of it or not, you are in the presence of Greatness. The King is closer to you than the air you breathe.

In one sense, everyone is in the presence of God since God is everywhere. But although He is all places at once (theologians call it omnipresence), this does not mean that all people have access to Him. We could say they don't have His ear.

As I write, the air in my room is filled with radio signals, scores of them. But at this moment I hear nothing. Silence is all about me. Why? Because the radio switch is turned off; the mechanism that picks up the signals is powerless. The signals are around me, but there's no connection. Signals are worthless unless they are picked up, interpreted and transmitted.

Similarly, God is everywhere. He is a witness to

every evil that is committed. He exists alongside of every particle of matter in the universe. His presence goes to the core of the earth and the farthest star.

But God does not respond to the prayers of all men. God told His chosen people He would not hear their prayers because of their unconfessed sin (Isa. 1:15). Nor does God have fellowship with people apart from His Son. Those who know Christ know the Father; those who do not know Jesus Christ do not know the Father. John wrote, "Whoever denies the Son does not have the Father; the one who confesses the Son has the Father also" (1 John 2:23, NASB). God can only be reached on one frequency: Jesus Christ.

Ever since creation, God has chosen a location where His presence has been especially displayed. For example, in the tabernacle He was in the Holy of Holies—the special dwelling place of the Most High.

In this age, God has come by means of the Holy Spirit to live within His people, the church (1 Cor. 6:19). He is readily accessible, available and close-by. But there is more. Because the sin barrier has been removed we have special access to the Father. We have been escorted to His presence.

In the New Testament there are three passages that teach that we have access to God (Rom. 5:2; Eph. 2:18; 3:12). In secular Greek the word *access* referred to the introduction of a speaker into the presence of the assembly, or of bringing a person to a king.

For years I thought that when Paul wrote "we have access . . . " he meant simply that we could pray whenever we want. We have a standing invitation to talk to God whenever we think it necessary. Of course, it means that, but much more besides.

Yes, we can pray to God whenever we wish, but the word *access* means that we are *already* in His presence.

Chrysostom, one of the church fathers, put it accurately, "The word doesn't describe our act, but His bringing us." Peter captured the idea, "For Christ also died for sins once for all, the just for the unjust in order that He might bring us to God, having been put to death in the flesh but made alive in the Spirit" (1 Peter 3:18, NASB). Christ has escorted us into the presence of God.

Think back to the days of the Old Testament, when the High Priest entered into the Holy of Holies once each year. Imagine his apprehension. He rehearsed his ritual, concentrating on every detail. He was afraid of being struck dead if he made one mistake. For a few moments, he was in the presence of the Lord of heaven and earth.

The moment Christ died on the cross a remarkable spectacle happened. "And Jesus uttered a loud cry, and breathed His last. And the veil of the temple was torn in two from top to bottom" (Mark 15:37-38, NASB). The thick veil was split down the middle, a sovereign miracle of God.

Why? To symbolize a profound truth: the barrier between God and man has been completely removed. As priests we not only can enter into the Holy of Holies, but we are already within the sanctuary. Our High Priest did not enter an earthly tabernacle like the one in the Old Testament era, but He entered into heaven to appear in the presence of God the Father for us (Heb. 9:24). He took us there with Him. We are seated at the right hand of God the Father, in the majestic presence of the Most High.

Three Levels of Fellowship
The ritual of the Old Testament tabernacle beautifully illustrates three classes of Christians, or three levels of spiritual growth. In the courtyard of the tabernacle

stood the brazen altar. Animal sacrifices were offered there for the forgiveness of sins. Many Christians never get beyond the brazen altar in their Christian experiences. To them, the Christian life means no more than the forgiveness of sin. They come repeatedly to Christ for forgiveness; their lives are characterized by the cycle of failure, confession, failure and confession.

There is a second stage of Christian experience. After one walked into the tabernacle he came to the holy place. This area contained three articles of furniture—the lampstand, the table of shewbread and the altar of incense. These articles symbolized Christ—the light of the world, the bread of life and the intercessor. Christians who come to this stage enjoy the presence of Christ and find Him satisfying. They understand that the goal of salvation is fellowship.

But finally, there is the Holy of Holies. As mentioned, the High Priest entered this area only one day a year, on the Day of Atonement. The priest entered with the blood and sprinkled that blood on the mercy seat. Now that the veil is torn from top to bottom, and we are in the Holy of Holies, we can enjoy the presence of the living God. This represents the highest stage in Christian experience: dwelling in the very presence of the Most High.

Living in God's Presence
I used to think that I had to enter God's presence through prayer usually beginning with the words, "Dear heavenly Father," and ending with "In Jesus' name, Amen." Special phrases, I thought, were the passwords into the Holy of Holies. My relationship with God became more practical when I realized I didn't have to move in and out of His presence. My entire life, crammed with routine activities, could be

lived within the privileged confines of the Almighty.

Of course, we ought to pray to God articulating our needs and offering our worship both privately and corporately. Each day should begin at the foot of the cross, humbly confessing our sins and acknowledging our needs for guidance and strength. Although posture is not important, I find that I am able to express my dependence better on my knees, a sign of our helplessness apart from the divine enablement. But once this fellowship has been established it can continue after we have risen from our knees to adjust to the world of schedules and interruptions. We need not leave God's presence when we say "Amen."

God will never be any closer to us than He is now. The poet was correct when he wrote:

Nearer, nearer, near to God
I cannot be;
For in the person of His Son
I am as near as He.

Dearer, dearer, dear to God
I cannot be;
For in the person of His Son,
I am as dear as He.

Author Unknown

Speaking, rejoicing, praising, complaining, discussing, all take place in the presence of God. A meeting, a temptation, an accident all happen at the right hand of God the Father where we are securely seated. When we live in an attitude of dependence, we learn the meaning of Paul's exhortation to "pray without ceasing" (1 Thes. 5:17).

After the funeral of a godly man, his daughter made this remark, "During the last few years of my dad's life, it seemed that he spent more time in heaven than he did on earth." He had learned the secret of resting in the heavenlies while enduring suffering on earth.

This is why a Christian need not fear crossing the unknown territory between life and death. Believers have already established legal residence in heaven. Sometimes when Americans go to Canada, they have difficulties crossing the border. In fact, some who intended to live in Canada have been denied visas. I happen to be a Canadian citizen, although I live in the United States. I have no difficulty in traveling to Canada; indeed, the government could not prevent my entry. The difference is citizenship, my legal rights.

At death we cross from one territory to another, but we'll have no trouble with visas. Our representative is already there, preparing for our arrival. As citizens of heaven, our entrance is incontestable.

Knowing God by Faith

Practicing the presence of God may sound like something only a mystic would do. We visualize a weird character walking aimlessly with his head in the clouds, oblivious to the world around him. He is constantly meditating, his face is expressionless, and without emotion. He is too "heavenly" to be concerned with anything else.

The assurance of God's presence is not based on feelings or a peculiar religious experience. We've all had special experiences with God, perhaps through prayer or Bible study. At such times we are confident that God is near, beside us, in us. But later that experience wears thin, our emotions subside, and the feelings are gone. God seems distant, uninterested and impersonal. And before we know it, we think that we have not met God at all. Why do we experience such ups and downs? Because we are taking our theology from our feelings, and not from the doctrinal teachings of the Bible.

A fisherman once told me that he felt closer to God in his boat on Sunday morning than he did in church. I do not doubt his sincerity, because experiencing nature firsthand can be exhilarating. I've often walked under the stars at night, overwhelmed by God's majestic handiwork. The Word of God agrees that "the heavens declare the glory of God" (Ps. 19:1).

But is the reality of God's presence dependent on a breath-taking experience with nature? What happens when the placid lake churns mercilessly in the path of a tornado? Or when the sun's light is darkened by a biting dust storm? Or when an earthquake shakes a village and a thousand people scream in terror?

In such moments God seems far away, even inaccessible. If His presence were dependent on our feelings, we would quickly assume that He had left us stranded. We dare not look to our subjective feelings for the assurance that God is near.

A girl who was hitchhiking through Europe decided to visit the L'Abri Fellowship in Switzerland. Although she was a Christian she was living a carnal, worldly life. At L'Abri she was restored to fellowship with God. As this young woman prepared to leave the beautiful Swiss Alps she was apprehensive, fearing that her experience with God would dissipate when she adjusted to the reality of life back in Chicago. When she expressed her fear to Dr. Francis Schaeffer, the founder and leader of L'Abri, his response was, "If you go back to Chicago and find out that God isn't real, then don't come back up here. If God isn't real in Chicago, then He isn't real up here either!"

Get the point? The presence of God is unrelated to location, whether in the beautiful Swiss Alps or the streets of Chicago. We may sometimes feel God is near, but He's just as near when we don't feel it.

How then do we know we are in His presence? We are dependent on His promises. Consider His words, "I will never desert you, nor will I ever forsake you" (Heb. 13:5, NASB). In the Greek New Testament this verse contains five negatives, stressing in the strongest possible language that God is committed to a policy of non-desertion. Other passages give similar assurance (Isa. 43:2; Matt. 28:20).

The writer of the Book of Hebrews encouraged believers to draw near with full assurance of faith (Heb. 10:19-22). Our knowledge of God comes by faith in His Word, not by our emotional stability or lack of it. We need not have a special antenna to pick up divine signals.

How far are you living from the sanctuary? In Christ, you have been brought to the throne room of the King. Yet sin can break your fellowship with Him.

Perhaps you've experienced failure. Maybe there are many frayed edges in your relationship with others and with God. But, through Christ all of our excuses have been removed. God does not meet us halfway. He came the whole distance so that no one has to be excluded.

If you sense a barrier between you and God, ask yourself: What has caused this? Sin? If so, confess it immediately, claiming the authority of 1 John 1:9. Or perhaps you have a feeling of inferiority. Remember that your hesitancy to draw near is not a mark of humility, but a proof of your unbelief—you refuse to accept Christ's sacrifice as sufficient for *you*. Listen to this exhortation, "Since therefore, brethren, we have confidence to enter the holy place by the blood of Jesus, by a new and living way which He inaugurated for us through the veil, that is, His flesh, and since we have a great priest over the house of God, let us draw near with a sincere heart in full assurance of faith" (Heb. 10:19-22, NASB).

Why not acknowledge God's presence and draw near to the King? We can be glad that Christ brought us into God's presence and left us there.

5

You Have a New Family: Sonship

What is a Christian? Ask the average believer and he will reply, "A sinner minus his sins." Of course, that is right—a Christian is one whose sins have been forgiven. But Christ did not die on the cross just so our sins could be forgiven, though that in itself would deserve our endless praise. Sin was a roadblock which God removed so that He could achieve some lofty goals in our lives. Specifically, we have been appointed to be sons of God.

The Apostle Paul says that God "predestinated us to adoption as sons, through Jesus Christ to Himself, according to the kind intention of His will" (Eph. 1:5, NASB). That word *predestinate* means to "mark out ahead of time." A surveyor, for example, goes into new territory to stake out roads, city blocks and new housing developments. When the people begin to arrive they build their homes according to the surveyor's master plan. Similarly, God planned that we would be chosen to receive the honored position of sonship.

If you were adopted into a king's family, you would have certain advantages. Status, wealth and special privileges come with such an honor. In this chapter we consider what it means to be adopted by God.

What Is Adoption?

The Greek word for *adoption* occurs five times in the writings of Paul (Rom. 8:15, 23; 9:4; Gal. 4:5; Eph. 1:5). Probably Paul referred to the Roman practice of adoption. Under Roman law a father had absolute power over his children so long as he and they lived. His authority was such that he could imprison, scourge or even kill them. In fact, a child could not possess anything; any inheritance willed to him became the property of his father.

Obviously, adoption was a serious step, so it was carried out by an impressive ritual. Twice the real father symbolically sold his son and bought him back; then he sold him a third time, and this time he did not buy him back. Then the adopting father had to go to the Roman magistrate and plead the case for adoption. When the act was completed, the son had all the rights of a legitimate son in his new family. The break with his old family was so complete that even all debts and obligations connected with his previous family were canceled out and abolished as if they had never existed.

Before we trusted Christ, we belonged to the family of Adam. We had his nature and were under its power. Characteristically, we reflected the attitudes and desires of our father: pride, anger, coveteousness, sensuality. Jesus even told the Pharisees that they were of their father the devil because they practiced deceit and hatred, traits of the wicked one (John 8:44).

We've all met people who believe that they will get to heaven because they are trying to be good. Such a theory of salvation is doomed because we are born as children of Adam. The best person, the most conscientious and moral, is still in the wrong family apart from faith in Christ. The issue is not so much how good or bad a person is, but whether he is in Adam's family or God's.

Through faith in Christ we are adopted into God's family. Our past spiritual debts are canceled; we are under the authority of a different Father. Added to this is a new inheritance and a whole new family tree, complete with a long roster of brothers and sisters in Christ.

What Is Sonship?

When a baby is born into a family, the infant is not capable of enjoying his inheritance. An infant can inherit a financial fortune, but it is impossible for him or her to use or profit from such riches. The child must grow up before he can spend his wealth. Laws spell out the minimum age at which a child can receive an inheritance. Maturity brings privileges. Paul wrote: "Now I say, as long as the heir is a child, he does not differ at all from a slave although he is owner of everything, but he is under guardians and managers until the date set by the father. So also we, while we were children, were held in bondage under the elemental things of the world" (Gal. 4:1-3, NASB).

When we are born into God's family, we do not have to mature spiritually before we can enjoy our status as sons (Gal. 4:5).

In Old Testament times, the nation Israel was like a child who needed rules and regulations to keep his conduct in check. The law pointed out sin and the need for divine grace. But now that Christ has come, God regards the believer as a mature son, not a little child. Unlike the nation Israel, we do not need a time of tutoring before we are introduced into the full blessing of sonship.

A new convert can enjoy the privileges of sonship. He immediately receives the family name, authority and resources. He must learn to apply God's gifts to his experience. Legally every son of God has the same status in the kingdom of God. As sons, the Father's blessing is now available to enjoy.

Privileges of Sonship

A sensitive father can never become indifferent to his son's needs. The bond of sonship is fastened with cords of love. That means that we become the focus of our Father's concern and special interest. John wrote, "See how great a love the Father has bestowed upon us, that we should be called children of God; and such we are" (1 John 3:1, NASB).

To be God's sons means we have His constant care and protection. God will never abandon us or put us up for adoption. We can never be involved in a child custody battle, for God holds all legal rights to our status and identity. We will never wake up and discover we are orphans.

Sometimes it is difficult to accept the fact of God's love. God does not demonstrate His love like an earthly father. For example, if you are sick and your human father could heal you, he would. Yet God often seems indifferent to our suffering. He watches us suffer from accidents, persecution and terminal illnesses. He could intervene, but chooses not to.

Does that mean He doesn't love us as much as a human father? No. He has promised His stedfast love to His children. We must accept the fact that God cares deeply about those in His family. Then why doesn't He prove His love? He does, but His values differ from ours. We value health; He values patience. We value comfort; He values peace. We value life without struggle; He values faith in the midst of struggle. Thus, though He loves us, He doesn't exempt us from the tragic heartaches of life. Never forget it: one privilege of being a son of God is that we come under the watchful care of a Father who knows what is best for us. He loves His adopted sons and daughters as He loves His only begotten Son, for He sees us *in Him* (Eph. 1:6). Nothing can separate us from His love.

Another privilege of sonship is the intimacy of family relationships. God no longer is distant, unapproachable and hidden. Paul taught that the spirit of adoption causes us to cry out "Abba, Father!" This term means "Papa," an expression of familiarity and affection.

A woman who was raised in an orphanage told me how she craved to be part of a family. As a teenager she walked the streets in the evenings, straining to look through windows just to see a family together. Often she saw them eating at a table or reclining in the living room. She would try to imagine what it would be like to really "belong." Finally, at the age of 20 and after being mistreated in several foster homes, she met Christian parents. They told her, "Don't call us Mr. and Mrs. _____, it's Dad and Mom." She was thrilled. At last the formalities of merely being an acquaintance or even a good friend were passed: now she moved right into the intimacy of the family circle.

Are you on the fringes of God's family circle? There is no reason to be satisfied with a tense relationship with your new family. If you feel excluded, it's because you have excluded yourself.

Often an illegitimate child struggles with self-acceptance. Those who are rejected by their parents have difficulty developing self-esteem; they feel guilty for simply being alive. They suffer from feelings of inferiority, depression and resentment. At least two steps are needed to rebuild their wounded emotions. First, they must choose to forgive those who have wronged them. Second, they must shift the focus of their attention away from themselves to their heavenly Father who accepts them independently of their background. David testified, "For my father and my mother have forsaken me, but the Lord will take me up" (Ps. 27:10, NASB).

This is more easily said than done. Emotional wounds do not heal easily. We need other believers to support us, encourage us and fill the vacuum left by neglect and rejection. But accepting our sonship is a big step in the right direction.

When Sons Misbehave

A friend of mine has said, "If you want to test someone's character, don't give him responsibility, give him privileges."

We are honored to be sons of God. What if we misbehave? When we do, God does what any father who loves his child does: He disciplines us.

Discipline is a proof of our sonship. In Hebrews we read, "For those whom the Lord loves He disciplines, and He scourges every son whom He receives. It is for discipline that you endure; God deals with you as with sons; for what son is there whom his father does not discipline? But if you are without discipline, of which all have become partakers, then you are illegitimate children and not sons" (Heb. 12:6-8, NASB).

Have you ever disciplined your neighbor's children? No, though you have probably wished you could. I heard one man recall how he and the neighbor's son mutilated a nearby garden when they were youngsters. The boy's father rushed outside, took his son by the arm and walked him calmly to the house for a sound spanking. "But what about Billy?" the boy asked. "He's not my responsibility," his father snapped, "but you are!"

What's the difference? Sonship. A father not only has a right to discipline his child, he has an obligation to do so. And our Father in heaven will not shirk His responsibility when His children misbehave.

God does not punish us for our sins, but He disciplines us for disobedience. The distinction is that punishment has the idea of satisfying justice for a crime. But Christ satisfied the Father's justice on the cross. So now God disciplines His sons by bringing problems and struggles into their lives so that they will deepen their relationship with Him. He is not angry with us, but disciplines us so that we can mature spiritually.

The Book of Hebrews was written to believers who were tempted to become discouraged because of persecution. They were on the verge of giving up out of sheer exhaustion. The writer reminded them that they should not give up, but endure hardship like Christ did (Heb. 12:2-4).

When we are disciplined we can respond in one of three ways. First, we can ignore it or worse, become bitter. Second, we can faint, or lose heart and give up in the trials of life. The writer of Hebrews warned against both such attitudes, "My son do not regard lightly the discipline of the Lord nor faint when you are reproved by Him" (12:5, NASB). Either way, we lose out spiritually.

But there is a third response, which is to profit from discipline and use it as a stepping-stone rather than a stumbling block. Notice how discipline cured the psalmist from his spiritual wanderings, "Before I was afflicted I went astray, but now I keep Thy word" (Ps. 119:67, NASB). Later in the passage, he admitted that God's discipline was best for him, "It is good for me that I was afflicted, that I may learn Thy statutes (v. 71, NASB).

A shepherd sometimes breaks the leg of a stubborn lamb that habitually wanders off. The shepherd knows that wolves pounce on animals that foolishly choose their own paths. Breaking the leg of the little lamb seems cruel, but then the shepherd can keep it close to him, and in the end the animal will learn obedience.

How does God discipline us? Sometimes through the natural consequences of our own disobedience; sometimes by piling one difficulty upon another. Often it is by forcing us to face our weaknesses, confess our sins, or ask others to forgive us.

This leads to a question which troubles many believers: should we interpret all of our problems as discipline for specific sins? The obvious answer is no. Those whose lives are filled with tragedy are not necessarily more sinful than those who seem to live in uninterrupted comfort. Job, you will recall, experienced calamity, not because he was wicked, but because he was righteous (Job 1:8).

Often there is no apparent connection between hardship and a specific sin. But it isn't necessary to know why God allows misfortune in order to profit from it. Just because we cannot pinpoint a special reason for the trial doesn't mean that God had no reason for allowing it. Although discipline is not usually welcomed, "yet to those who have been trained by it, afterwards it yields the peaceful fruit of righteousness" (Heb. 12:11, NASB). Circumstances or the trials of life do not determine our attitudes. It is our reactions to them that shape our lives.

Living Up to the Family Name

You've seen two children playing together. One asks the other, "What does your dad do?" The other answers, "He's a preacher." There is a long pause and then, "I didn't know you were a preacher's kid. I always thought a preacher's kid would be different than you are."

What if your neighbors discovered that you were a king's son or daughter? Or that you had been adopted by the God of the universe? Would you be a credit to the family name?

If a man says, "My father is Mr. Jones," you look at his face to see if you can see any resemblance to his father. So when a believer says, "I am a son of God," we should expect that his life will have at least some trace of the character of God.

Everything that God brings into our lives is directed to one purpose: that we might be conformed to the image of Christ. We often quote Romans 8:28, "And we know that God causes all things to work together for good to those who love God, to those who are called according to His purpose" (NASB). But what is the good to which everything works? It is to be conformed to Christ's image. God has a program of character development for each one of us. He wants others to look at our lives and say, "He walks with God, for he lives like Christ."

What character traits does God want His children to develop? Love, joy, peace, patience, kindness, goodness, faithfulness, gentleness and self-control (Gal. 5:22-23). These should be our reactions to the circumstances and trials of life.

Sometimes parents admonish their children, "Remember that whatever you do reflects on the family." If a child is rebellious, that advice can backfire. Such children have been known to deliberately sin just to hurt their parents. But a child who loves his parents will try to please them. A young man told me it was easier for him to resist temptation when he remembered that he could not betray his parents' values.

If you are a believer, your actions reflect on God. That's why one of my professors in seminary used to say, "If you backslide, God has more to lose than you do!"

Paul lamented that the Jews of his time were living hypocritical lives and that God's name was being maligned because of them: "For the name of God is blasphemed among the Gentiles because of you" (Rom. 2:24, NASB).

God's eagerness to identify Himself with His people is sometimes frightening. When I take a long look at some believers I know, then take a self-inventory, I think that God's reputation in the world is sagging just a bit.

But Christ is not ashamed to call us His brethren (Heb. 2:11). For all our faults and imperfections, Christ is prepared to stick with us *without shame.* Yet I know Christians who feel uncomfortable when they bow their heads to pray in a restaurant. Others prefer that their neighbors not know that they are followers of the Lord Jesus Christ.

I'm told that Alexander the Great had an encounter with one of his soldiers, a man who had fled the scene of a battle. Alexander questioned the man who sheepishly admitted his cowardice. The famous Greek general concluded his interrogation by asking, "What is your name?" The soldier replied, "Alexander, sir."

With that Alexander the Great became enraged. He shook the soldier. Then lifting him by the scruff of his neck shouted, "Your name is Alexander? *Then either change your character or change your name!*"

If you were accused of being a son of God, would there be enough evidence to convict you?

6

You Have Spiritual Power: The Holy Spirit

Several years ago when archaeologists entered the tombs beneath the Egyptian pyramids, they discovered containers of grain buried beside the Pharoahs. The researchers carefully took the grain from the ancient vessels, and planted it in moist, warm soil. Incredibly, it grew! The life within the kernels remained imprisoned for 3000 years, until placed in the right conditions for growth.

So it is with the Holy Spirit. We as believers receive the gift of the Holy Spirit the moment we accept Christ as Saviour (Rom. 8:9). But this is no guarantee that the Spirit will be free to express His power in our lives until some conditions are met. Christ taught, "Truly, truly, I say to you, unless a grain of wheat falls into the earth and dies, it remains by itself alone; but if it dies, it bears much fruit (John 12:24, NASB).

Some Christians are apprehensive about a study of

the Holy Spirit. They believe that if they yield to the Spirit, they might become fanatics or speak in strange languages. Or worse, they believe that the Spirit's work is not important to their lives. Thus they attempt to bypass this special gift, the means by which God comes to live within us. Like the kernels of grain in the pyramid, they have life but there is no evidence of it.

Let's begin with some of the basic biblical teachings about the Holy Spirit, and learn how the Spirit's energy can be experienced in our lives.

Indwelling of the Spirit

The moment we accept Christ as Saviour, God creates a new nature within us; it is a capacity for righteousness. "Therefore, if any man is in Christ, he is a new creature; the old things passed away; behold, new things have come" (2 Cor. 5:17, NASB). Other passages speak of the "new man" (Eph. 4:24; Col. 3:9). Christ called it a new birth (John 3:3-7). This new nature is created by God. The Holy Spirit gives us the ability to put off the old nature with its deceptions and habitually live in His strength.

Since the Day of Pentecost, believers never have to ask for the Holy Spirit. He lives within us so that we can have communion with God (John 14:23). Any doubt about this can be cleared up by examining the Scriptures. Paul definitely taught that those who did not have the Spirit were unsaved, "Now if any man have not the Spirit of Christ, he is none of His" (Rom. 8:9). Even more clearly, he wrote to the church at Corinth (a mixture of believers among whom many were worldly), "Or do you not know that your body is a temple of the Holy Spirit who is in you, whom you have from God, and that you are not your own?" (1 Cor. 6:19, NASB)

In Old Testament times, God's presence was localized in a special way in the tabernacle. The Shekinah glory descended after the tabernacle was completed and later the glory of God descended at the dedication of Solomon's temple.

Since Pentecost, God no longer lives in a temple made with hands, but His presence has been transferred to the body of each believer. That's why Paul wrote that our bodies are temples of the Holy Spirit. That word *temple,* is the word used to refer to the Holy of Holies, the place where God Himself dwelt. Paul added, "As God said, I will dwell in them and walk among them: and I will be their God, and they shall be My people" (2 Cor. 6:16, NASB).

The Holy Spirit is not a gift we must beg to receive. He comes without reservation to every believer. We need not hold "tarrying meetings," beseeching the Spirit to fall upon us. The message of the New Testament is that He already indwells us, awaiting the conditions that enable Him to work.

What happens when we sin? We grieve the Spirit, but He does not desert us. In the Old Testament, the Holy Spirit did on occasion leave individuals because of sin (1 Sam. 16:14). But there are no such references since Pentecost, when the Holy Spirit came in a new way, and for a new ministry (John 14:17). Now, Christ has promised that the Holy Spirit will abide with us forever (John 14:16).

Baptism of the Spirit

All believers are *indwelt* by the Holy Spirit, but some Christians are not convinced that all believers have been baptized by the Holy Spirit. Some teach that when a believer receives "the baptism," he will speak in foreign languages or unintelligible sounds. Others seek to be baptized by the Spirit to receive spiritual power.

Part of the problem is due to the terminology used. Bible teachers sometimes confuse the baptism of the Spirit with the filling of the Spirit; others speak of two baptisms, one done by the Holy Spirit and another done by Christ. Little wonder that many Christians feel perplexed and uncomfortable discussing the baptism of the Holy Spirit.

Summarizing the issues is not easy. Two verses in the New Testament speak clearly of the baptism of the Spirit. John the Baptist predicted Christ would baptize with the Holy Spirit and with fire (Matt. 3:11). Later, Christ reminded His disciples, "For John baptized with water, but you shall be baptized with the Holy Spirit not many days from now" (Acts 1:5, NASB). This promise was fulfilled on the Day of Pentecost, when the believers were baptized with the Spirit, and the body of Christ was formed.

Paul wrote, "For by one Spirit we were all baptized into one body, whether Jews or Greeks, whether slaves or free, and we were all made to drink of one Spirit" (1 Cor. 12:13, NASB). Observe that all believers have been baptized with the Holy Spirit. Paul did not limit the baptism to those in Corinth who were spiritual. He taught that this work of God was universal among all believers. Significantly, neither here nor in any other passage did Paul ask believers to seek the baptism. This is in marked contrast to some ministers today who urge believers to "get the baptism" by yieldedness and willingness to speak in strange tongues. But in the New Testament there is no such exhortation.

If all believers have received the baptism of the Spirit as Paul taught, then the gift of tongues must not be proof of the baptism. The reason is obvious: all believers do not speak in tongues. Those who believe that speaking in tongues is the sign of the baptism are aware of this powerful argument. Clearly, Paul taught all believers have been baptized by the Spirit, yet it is clear that all believers do not speak in tongues (1 Cor. 12:30).

Why then do some still insist that we seek the baptism? They think that all believers have been baptized by the Spirit into the body of Christ, but not all believers have the baptism experienced by the early church. This, it is held, is a baptism done by Jesus Christ who puts us into the sphere of the Holy Spirit. Since the early believers spoke in tongues (Acts 2), it is assumed that the gift of tongues is the sign of this baptism.

This is why some people speak of the baptism *in* the Spirit, and another baptism *by* the Spirit. They believe that Acts 1:5 should be translated "in the Spirit," whereas 1 Corinthians 12:13 should be translated "by the Spirit." All this may seem rather technical, but its implications have far reaching consequences. If all believers have one baptism but there is another some don't have, then presumably, they ought to seek this special baptism.

Two Baptisms or One?

Are there two baptisms—one done by the Holy Spirit, the other done by Christ? The answer is *no*. For one thing, the Greek preposition in Acts 1:5 and 1 Corinthians 12:13 is the same. It can be translated either as *in* or *by*, but whatever translation we adopt must be consistent. So to say we are baptized *in* the Spirit is fine, as long as we do not make an artificial distinction between this and some other baptism *by* the Spirit. The point is that Acts 1:5 and 1 Corinthians 12:13 refer to the same act.

Since the Scriptures teach that this baptism makes us members of the body of Christ, it is probably best to translate the Greek preposition with the word *by*. The Holy Spirit would then be the agent of the baptizing; it is He that places us into the body of Christ.

Admittedly, Christ predicted that He would baptize us, but the means would be the Holy Spirit. The baptism of the Spirit takes place at the will of Christ. He is the baptizer, but the means He uses is the Holy Spirit. Christ sent the Holy Spirit, and He fulfills Christ's ministry (John 16:14-15).

Consistency demands that we not divide believers into two camps, those who have one baptism of the Spirit but not another. The baptism of the Spirit is given to every believer without distinction.

But didn't the gift of tongues accompany the baptism in the Book of Acts? True, the gift of tongues occurred on the same day as the baptism of the Spirit. But the New Testament does not teach that this association will continue, for one good reason: the gift of tongues was given not as a sign of the baptism, but as a sign that God was now broadening His work to include the Gentiles, represented by various languages, into His program. Tongues occurred as proof that the gospel would now be spoken not merely in Hebrew, but in the languages of Gentiles. Isaiah predicted that the day would come when God would speak to the Jews through the stammering lips of Gentiles. Tongues, Paul says, were a sign to the unbelieving nation that the era of the Gentiles had come (1 Cor. 14:21-22). Tongues are not a sign of the baptism of the Spirit. We can conclude that every believer has been baptized by the Spirit, and is a member of Christ's body. This union with Him is the basis for our new walk with Jesus Christ. The baptism of the Spirit unites believers to one another, and collectively unites us to Christ. Our relationship is so direct that Christ feels our sorrows and joys.

Remember the days of persecution in the Book of Acts? The infant church was facing insurmountable odds. Believers were thrown into prison, beaten and killed. Leading the onslaught was none other than Saul of Tarsus, a young Jew who thought he was doing God a favor. Perhaps since everyone was too afraid to witness to him, the Lord Himself spoke to Saul from heaven. His words were, "Saul, Saul, why are you persecuting Me?" (Acts 9:4, NASB) Persecution against the church is persecution against Christ.

The hurt we feel, Christ feels; the rejection we experience, He experiences. This close relationship takes place because the Spirit has inseparably joined us to the Lord.

Walking in the Spirit

What does it mean to be filled with the Holy Spirit? Does it mean that we smile all the time? Should all who walk in the Spirit look alike or act alike?

To walk in the Spirit is to have Christlike responses to the experiences of life. The fruit of the Spirit essentially involves our attitudes toward the many and varied circumstances that we all face. To be Spirit filled means that we are not controlled by what happens on the outside but by what is happening on the inside.

How do we learn to tap the Spirit's resources? First, we must not "grieve the Holy Spirit of God, by whom you were sealed for the day of redemption" (Eph. 4:30, NASB). The Spirit is grieved when we tolerate sin in our lives.

After he admonished us not to grieve the Spirit, Paul listed the sins that rob us of spiritual power. First is bitterness. Bitterness often develops within the context of strained family relationships. Divorces, harsh parents, and unfair treatment generate bitterness. If you are the victim of such feelings, you must *choose* to forgive whoever has wronged you. Forgiveness is not an emotion, it is a decision of the will.

Next, Paul listed anger and wrath. We cannot excuse our outbursts of anger, blaming the frustrations of life for our tantrums. God knows that we will become angry, but He wants us to focus on the problem that anger causes. The Holy Spirit is to control us, so that when we become angry, we do not sin (Eph. 4:26). These are examples of the kinds of sin that hamper the Spirit's ministry.

There is a second step we must take to be filled with the Spirit. We must choose to live by faith. The control of the Spirit is not based on our feelings which fluctuate and often mislead us. Rather, it is based on committing ourselves to God by faith. The just shall *live* by faith (Hab. 2:4).

Here's the way Paul put it, "As you therefore have received Christ Jesus the Lord, so walk in Him" (Col. 2:6, NASB). Most Christians understand that salvation comes by faith, apart from feelings. But they think that the Spirit controlled life requires some type of mystical experience—a feeling, a surge of power, or being overcome by waves of love. Those experiences are usually not around when you need them. What you need is spiritual power, independent of feelings, experiences or circumstances. That comes when we give each day to God and anticipate His blessing.

We must choose to depend on the Holy Spirit for power, just as we depend on Christ's death for forgiveness. The basis for our forgiveness is Christ's death; the basis of the gift of the Holy Spirit is Christ's ascension (John 7:39; Acts 2:33). Just as we receive forgiveness by faith and we prove our faith by thanking God for Christ's death, so we accept the ministry of the Holy

Spirit by faith and thank God for Christ's glorification. Forgiveness and the work of the Holy Spirit are both accepted by saying thank-you to God (1 Thes. 5:18).

Let me illustrate it this way. If you bought a two-volume book and carelessly left one volume at the store, what would you do? You would return to the store and get the other volume. Since you paid for both, you need not be content with just one. Similarly, Christ's death which gives us forgiveness and His ascension which is the basis for the Spirit's coming, are all part of our salvation. Both have been provided and paid for. They become ours by faith when we say thank-you to God for what He has *already* done.

Remember this: the Holy Spirit is more willing to control us than we are willing to let Him. We need never think that we must overcome the Spirit's reluctance. He will empower any believer who is willing to remove the obstacles to spiritual growth and begin each day with faith in the Spirit's presence and ministry.

7

You Are a Precious Possession: God's Inheritance

You are sitting at home one evening when the doorbell rings. The man at the front door identifies himself as an attorney who has come to find the relative of a deceased person. He asks questions about your mother, your uncle, and an aunt. Finally, the lawyer requests a copy of your birth certificate. Satisfied with your answers and the legal proof of your identity, he says, "I'm happy to inform you that you have a large inheritance, primarily of jewels, diamonds and other precious stones, worth about two million dollars!" Your mother's uncle in San Francisco has died; the inheritance is yours.

Moments later, the attorney discusses the details of shipping the jewels to your home in Chicago. How will you transport your treasures? Not by the U.S. mail service, to be sure. Nor would you ask a friend to bring it to you. On the spot you decide to fly there personally and be on hand when your inheritance is distributed. Then you either make special arrangements to have it insured and shipped under private security, or you fly back with a heavy briefcase trying desperately to look poverty-stricken.

Those jewels represent years of investment. When you return you will put your valuables in the bank before you decide what to do with the rest of your life.

The amount of care we give an object is always determined by its value. We drive a new car into the garage; the old one can stay parked on the street. Cheap jewelry can be put anywhere in the house; our diamonds are tucked carefully away, and if we have any to spare, they are put into a vault.

If your house caught on fire and you had three minutes to salvage your belongings, what would you take? You'd begin by making sure no people would be trapped inside—all the children would have to be accounted for. Then you'd grab any expensive jewelry, some irreplaceable pictures, and a few other precious possessions as you escape through the flaming doorway.

Belonging to God

God has only one set of valuables. Needless to say, they are not diamonds, mink coats or eight-track stereos. Before the world goes up in smoke, God will snatch up only one commodity: people. Although all men everywhere shall become immortal, only one group is called His special possession: believers.

Do you realize you are the most important asset God will ever own? He has not invested in stocks and bonds, gold or silver. He has, at high cost, bought some property which He intends to keep forever. This property, composed of believers since time began, is His inheritance. He plans to guard it with meticulous care.

That's what Paul meant when he prayed that the believers at Ephesus might know "the riches of the glory of His inheritance in the saints" (Eph. 1:18, NASB). Notice what Peter wrote, "But you are a chosen race, a royal priesthood, a holy nation, a people for God's own possession, that you may proclaim the excellencies of Him who has called you out of darkness into His marvelous light" (1 Peter 2:9, NASB). Simply put, you are God's property.

What is our price tag? Not silver and gold, but the sacrifice of the Son of God. "Knowing that you were not redeemed with perishable things like silver or gold from your futile way of life inherited from your forefathers, but with precious blood, as of a lamb unblemished and spotless, the blood of Christ" (1 Peter 1:18-19, NASB).

The word *redeem* means "to buy out of the marketplace." We were in bondage to sin, fulfilling its desires and lusts. Christ freed us by paying a ransom, the sacrifice of Himself.

Remember that story of the boy who lost his boat? He had been sailing it along the edge of a small lake, when a sudden gust of wind blew it further than he could reach. Minutes later it was drifting across the lake. For a couple of days he searched carefully along the opposite side of the lake for the little boat, but couldn't find it.

Weeks later while walking past a store in his small town, he noticed his own boat for sale in the window! The boy told the proprietor that the boat was his and that he wanted to take it home. But to his great disappointment, he was told he would have to buy it, even though it had been his. After he paid for it he exclaimed, "Now it's twice mine!"

By virtue of creation, the whole human race belongs to God. But the fall of man necessitated that we had to be purchased. The sacrifice of Christ was a payment made to God the Father. The cruel death of Christ was our ticket to freedom. Think of how precious we must be to God.

If the value of an article is dependent upon the price paid for it, Christ's death made our value skyrocket. Let no one say we are worthless. God is not a foolish speculator; He would never invest in worthless property.

Sometimes believers, out of a sense of humility, degrade themselves: "I'm really nobody, just the dirt in between the toes of the body of Christ." Such false humility is not a credit to God. Christ would not have died for worms, or for the scum of the earth. Of course, it is true that we are depraved sinners, totally unable to find an ounce of credible righteousness within ourselves, but we *are* also human beings, created in God's image.

The most obscure believer, even the least successful among us, can hold his head high, look tomorrow square in the eye and exclaim, "I am special to the God of the universe!" You might not want to honk your horn if you love Jesus, but you could at least put a smile on your face.

Think of what the nation Israel meant to God. The tribes were given allotments in the land, but as for God, His portion was His people (Deut. 32:9). Since one of the most sensitive parts of the body is the eye, we involuntarily protect our eyes with our hands, or quickly turn aside from flying objects or particles of dust. Moses wrote that God guarded Israel as the pupil of

His eye (Deut. 32:10). The Most High does not play fast and loose with His inheritance.

Another figure of speech communicates the same idea. When eaglets are afraid to leave the nest, the mother eagle sometimes pushes them out. If they cannot fly and begin to fall, the mother swoops beneath them so they can land on her back. They then ride nonstop back to the nest. This is what God does, "like an eagle that stirs up its nest, that hovers over its young, He spread His wings and caught them, He carried them on His pinions" (Deut. 32:11, NASB). Did God care when His people were hungry? Was He concerned when the water they drank was bitter? Yes, God is more concerned than an eagle for its young.

Our Security

Can you be sure your inheritance will not be lost? Can God be sure His will not be? Definitely. He will never allow a thief to steal us or an imposter to rename us. Nor will we be lost in the shuffle. We are His forever.

Suppose you were a shepherd, entrusted with the care of 100 sheep. One night you come home with only 98; the next night it's 93. You would be the laugh of the town. No other shepherd would entrust his sheep to your care. Sarcastic comments would pass behind your back. So much for your reputation.

Sometimes sheep follow false paths made by thieves who intend to capture the stray animals. At other times they are strong willed, downright stubborn. They strike out on their own, determined to investigate forbidden terrain. The shepherd brings them back to the flock. A good shepherd doesn't lose his sheep.

Christ taught, "And this is the will of Him who sent Me, that of all that He has given Me I lose nothing, but raise it up on the last day" (John 6:39, NASB). Jesus was committed to fulfilling the will of the Father, namely, to keep all the sheep the Father gave Him. Thus Christ promised, "My sheep hear My voice and I know them and they follow me; and I give eternal life to them, and they shall never perish; and no one shall snatch them out of My hand. My Father, who has given them to Me is greater than all; and no one is able to snatch them out of the Father's hand" (John 10:27-29, NASB).

Furthermore, the gift of the Holy Spirit is a pledge that God will bring us to heaven. "In Him, you also, after listening to the message of truth, the gospel of your salvation—having also believed, you were sealed in Him with the Holy Spirit of promise, who is given as a pledge of our inheritance, with a view to the redemption of God's own possession, to the praise of His glory" (Eph. 1:13-14, NASB).

The Spirit is a seal, a guarantee that we are secure and that we will reach our destination. In early times when a king sent an important letter, it was sealed with wax, then stamped with the king's signet. Only the recipient was authorized to break the seal and open the letter. When it arrived, the unbroken seal was a guarantee that the letter had not been tampered with; it arrived exactly in the condition it had been sent. In our case, God is both the sender and the recipient. He sends us to heaven and is on hand for our arrival. Only God could break the seal, but He has promised not to do so. We are sealed for the day of redemption (Eph. 4:30).

The Holy Spirit is also called the earnest or pledge. One incident in my childhood illustrates the meaning. My father decided to buy a grain harvester from a neighbor. After the deal was agreed upon verbally, my father gave the man $45 to confirm the agreement. When my dad asked whether this was enough, the man replied, "As far as I'm concerned $5 binds the deal as securely as $100." The point is that earnest money is a pledge that the transaction will be completed.

The gift of the Spirit makes God's agreement binding. By giving us part of our inheritance now, God is obligated to give us the rest later.

Paul said that the Spirit is given "with a view to the redemption of God's own possession, to the praise of His glory" (Eph. 1:14, NASB). We are given the pledge, the earnest, because we are God's property. We are secure not because we can keep ourselves, but because we are owned by God, the One who is qualified to protect His investment.

I'm aware that some teach that we can undo the work that God has begun in us. We can choose—so the argument goes—to completely break our relationship with God and be lost forever. This is not an issue that can be settled in this chapter, since that would involve a study of many different passages and the discussion of many arguments. But as we learned in the chapter on election, God initiates salvation and He will complete it. He is well able to take care of His assets. Yes, we like sheep may rebel and follow false paths, but the Shepherd will see to it that we are in the fold before nightfall.

God's Care for His Estate

Since we belong to God, He takes an active part in directing every one of us. He does this not merely for our own good, but because His honor is at stake. David wrote, "He restores my soul; He guides me in paths of righteousness for His name's sake" (Ps. 23:3, NASB). Wayward, disobedient and forgetful as we are, our welfare is His responsibility.

God is sensitive about His reputation. When Moses was on Mount Sinai, the Israelites succumbed to idolatry by making a golden calf to worship. Aaron led the rebellion, fashioning the idol with his own hands. God told Moses what was happening down in the valley, "Now let Me alone, that My anger may burn against them, and that I may destroy them; and I will make of you a great nation" (Ex. 32:10, NASB).

Moses did not fall for the temptation to make himself great. Rather, he reminded God that His own reputation would be defamed if He destroyed Israel. The Egyptians, Moses said, would interpret God's action to mean that He had misled His own people. The pagans would say that God brought His people into the wilderness to destroy them. Furthermore, it would appear as if God led the people out of one land but was incapable of bringing them into another.

God was pleased with Moses' reminder. Not that the Almighty had momentarily forgotten that His honor was at stake, but He is pleased when our requests put His reputation above our own. God delights in taking care of His people so that no one will accuse Him of neglect.

Some of our anxieties cease when we remember this. As God's real estate, nothing happens to us without His consent, and under His watchful supervision.

One person acknowledged, "I was always afraid of getting cancer until I realized that this body was God's, not mine. That helped me to remember that God has a right to do as He wishes with His property."

We've all met people who have let their property and land deteriorate. Dilapidated houses and yards strewn with trash populate some neighborhoods. Property that could skyrocket in price declines because of a lack of initiative, money or interest. Perhaps the owners have no idea how valuable their property is, and therefore, don't care what it looks like. An investor would be foolish to purchase real estate in the area unless he knew it could be improved so that its value would not skid to new lows.

Does God allow His property to deteriorate? In one sense it may appear so, since our bodies which belong to Him eventually become weak and decrepit. God's inheritance is susceptible to disease, the victim of cruel circumstances and subject to accidents. Believers have as much misfortune as unbelievers. Outwardly, at least, it seems as if belonging to God through redemption doesn't have many advantages.

But let's remember that God's intention is not to keep His chosen ones from hardships. Nor is He primarily concerned about keeping us healthy and well preserved. He did not even do this for His own Son. This is not, however, an expression of His disinterest. Nor does it reflect unfavorably on His ability to keep up His property.

God's interests lie in a different direction. Contrary to what the cosmetic industry would have us believe, the most important part of us is the part that no one ever sees. God is not interested in giving us a face lift to increase our value. All the beauty aids on earth, necessary as we might think they are, cannot increase our value in the eyes of the Almighty. Our worth is neither increased or diminished by our outer appearance.

God's concern is for the inner man, the individual human personality which He intends to develop. This doesn't mean that the body is unimportant; it is so valuable that God will resurrect it in the last day. But since our bodies are part of this decaying world, God's primary purpose is to equip us to live in the incorruptible world to come. Paul wrote, "Therefore we do not lose heart, but though our outer man is decaying, yet our inner man is being renewed day by day. For momentary, light affliction is producing for us an eternal weight of glory far beyond all comparison, while we look not at the things which are seen, but at the things which are not seen; for the things which are seen are temporal, but the things which are not seen are eternal (2 Cor. 4:16-18, NASB).

Contrary to appearance, God is not an absentee landlord. He uses all of His resources to protect His investment, and develop it for His and our future glory. The process might be painful but it is accomplished by the One who gives His inheritance around-the-clock attention.

8

You Serve a New Master: Identification with Christ

Have you ever tried to break a sinful habit? If so, you know that it takes more than sheer will power. Worry, anger, pride and lust are too powerful for us to conquer. Add to this a host of more subtle sins and we know that apart from God we are in deep trouble.

Jesus Christ has already provided a basis for the personal victory of all believers. We must be convinced that He had us in mind when He died on the cross and ascended into heaven.

I can hear you say, "But you don't know me—I've struggled with temptation and have lost so many times that I've had to admit that personal victory is an illusion, a false hope perpetuated by professional clergymen."

If you think that way, here is a small word of comfort: all of us have felt like that at times. No honest believer has escaped the disillusionment of personal spiritual defeat. But thank God that each of us *can* also drink from the refreshing streams of victory.

Winning the Battle

The first step toward victory is to believe that deliverance from personal sin is possible. Charles Finney wrote, "The Gospel, as a matter of fact, has often, not only temporarily, but permanently and perfectly, overcome every form of sin in different individuals. Who has not seen the most beastly lusts, drunkenness, lasciviousness, and every kind of abomination, long indulged and fully ripe, entirely and forever slain by the power of the grace of God?" Regardless of what your particular vice might be, you can take comfort in the fact that someone else faced a temptation as fierce as yours and successfully overcame it. As Paul wrote, "No temptation has overtaken you but such as is common to man; and God is faithful, who will not allow you to be tempted beyond what you are able, but with the temptation will provide the way of escape also, that you may be able to endure it" (1 Cor. 10:13, NASB).

There is no victory without a battle. In fact, God allows temptation so that we will benefit from the struggle. The Holy Spirit drove Christ into the wilderness to be tempted of the devil. Why? So Christ could face the challenge of Satan directly and forever settle any doubts about His allegiance to the Father. Similarly, God, though He does not tempt us, allows temptation so we have a clear opportunity to choose for Him. It's God's way of testing our loyalty—do we love Him more than our sinful pleasures?

But we must begin by believing that victory is possible. Charles Wesley was right when he wrote:

He breaks the power of canceled sin
He sets the prisoner free

His blood can make the vilest clean
His blood availed for me.

Second, we must constantly enlarge our understanding of what Christ has already done. When Paul prayed for the church at Ephesus it was that the eyes of their heart might be enlightened, that they might understand " . . . the surpassing greatness of His power toward us who believe" (Eph. 1:19, NASB).

The believers didn't need any more blessings, since they had them all in Christ (Eph. 1:3). They *did* need discernment and understanding to apply Christ's work to their lives.

There is one more benefit we receive when we accept Christ as Saviour. It is that our relationship with Adam has been broken and we are now *in Christ,* identified with the risen Lord. This transition from Adam to Christ is the basis for breaking our sinful habits.

We were born under the authority of sin. Adam's sin was credited to us; we were guilty simply because we are human beings (Rom. 5:12). Added to this is the painful fact that we were born with a corrupt sin nature. Like it or not, we were under the rule of sin, and were forced to obey its lusts and deceptions.

We received wages for our service: moral entanglements, guilt, perpetual slavery and spiritual death. Of course, these rewards are usually not immediate. We always sin on the installment plan. The bills come in later. But come they will, for sin pays handsomely, relentlessly.

However, at the moment of salvation we were transferred to a new relationship. We have a new master, a new identity and a radically different destiny. The wages are different too. "For the wages of sin is death, but the free gift of God is eternal life in Christ Jesus our Lord" (Rom. 6:23, NASB).

Years ago when slavery was officially abolished in Jamaica, some of the slaves, particularly those in remote areas, did not know of their freedom. Several years after their release had been announced, hundreds of them still continued in their drudgery, oblivious to the fact that a new relationship between them and the government had been established. They were no longer officially under the tyranny of slavery, but they didn't know it.

When Paul wrote about our being "in Christ," he meant that our ties to Adam have been legally severed. Of course, we can still obey the dictates of sin. We can become victims of sinful habits, but we don't have to. Only ignorance and unbelief can keep us bound to our former life-styles.

This new relationship of being "in Christ" was announced by the Lord to His disciples in the upper room, "In that day you shall know that I am in My Father, and you in Me and I in you" (John 14:20, NASB). This promise was fulfilled on the Day of Pentecost and is now the inheritance of every believer.

Obviously, there is no physical connection between us and Christ, but we are inseparably joined to Him because our past ties have been dissolved and a new relationship has been established. Christ is not only in us, but we are *in Him*. Before we spell out how this should affect our conduct, let's take a closer look at what Paul says about our position in Christ.

Identifying with Christ

The Apostle Paul never lost the wonder of the fact that believers are "in Christ." More than 100 times in his writings he used this expression. Almost every exhortation, every plea for godliness is based on this special relationship with Jesus Christ.

Let's consider one of the most familiar passages that speaks of our union with Christ. Paul wrote, "knowing this, that our old self was crucified with Him, that our body of sin might be done away with, that we should no longer be slaves to sin" (Rom. 6:6, NASB). Many interpret the phrase "our old self" to refer to our sin nature. That would mean that our sin nature was judged at the cross, or to put it more strongly, our sin nature was put to death at the cross.

However, a problem arises when we interpret the passage in this way. How can we say that our sin nature has been crucified when in fact it is very much alive? The Bible does not teach that we can become sinless in this life. If it did, it would be difficult to reconcile the Bible with my experience and the lives of honest Christians. What then, did Paul mean when he wrote, "knowing this, that our old self was crucified with him"?

The expression "old self" (the King James translates it "old man") refers to the man we used to be in Adam. This is consistent with the contrast Paul draws between Adam and Christ in the previous chapter (Rom. 5:12-21). How did we get into Adam? By birth. How do we get out? By death; not a physical death, but by cutting off all legal ties to our past life of sin. Then we are free to enter a different family, with new leadership and new rule. This is precisely what the death of Christ accomplished. So then our ties to Adam have been severed and a new relationship has been established. To reckon ourselves dead to sin means that we acknowledge that we are not obligated to obey the sin nature any longer.

Two consequences follow. First, we are now morally obligated to obey Christ, rather than live under the tyranny of sin. Paul used the human body to illustrate what being identified with Christ means (Eph. 5:23).

He is the head, we are the hands, legs, eyes and toes. One of the most poignant sights is a person who cannot control the parts of his body. His muscles act spasmodically, with no purpose. What a picture of believers who refuse to submit to the One who is the Head of all and gives us life and purpose.

In 1951 President Truman removed Douglas MacArthur from his command in the Pacific. A new general was then appointed to succeed him. The soldiers were obligated to switch their allegiance. Some of them out of loyalty to MacArthur may have refused to obey the new general. But that would have been deliberate disobedience to the president.

We now have a new Boss, though some of us may not have switched our allegiance to Him yet. A double-minded person is still not convinced that obedience to Christ is better than obedience to Adam (our sin nature), or else he foolishly believes he can obey two masters at the same time. Such double-mindedness causes instability, and breeds spiritual cripples (James 1:8).

Second, since we are "in Christ," the power of sin has *already* been broken in the believer's life. We don't have to obey our sinful natures or Satan. We must insist on our rights as members of a new body, individuals with direct ties to Jesus Christ.

Breaking the power of sin does not come by merely yielding ourselves to God, even though this is the first step. Rather, it comes by shifting our attention to Jesus Christ and our relationship with Him in His death and resurrection. The victory which He won on the cross is transmitted to us by the Holy Spirit, who then supplies the power needed to live new lives. But this only happens when we accept our identification with Christ by faith.

Remember Joshua's war with Amalek recorded in Exodus 17? Moses asked Joshua to choose an army and tackle Amalek head-on in the valley. Moses took his staff, a symbol of leadership, and climbed to the top of the mountain. Aaron and Hur went with him. The text says, "So it came about when Moses held his hand up, that Israel prevailed, and when he let his hand down, Amalek prevailed" (v. 11, NASB).

Where was the real battle going on—in the valley or on the mountaintop? The answer is obvious. Moses' raised hands were symbolic of intercession. When he became weary, Aaron and Hur supported his hands; if not, Joshua would have lost. The issue of defeat or victory was being settled on the mountaintop, not between the soldiers in the valley.

Similarly, we learn to become victorious as we enlarge our understanding of the work of Christ on the cross. Every struggle we meet was faced there successfully. If we are in Christ, we are not obligated to serve the flesh; rather, we are commanded to serve the living God. Strength for that task is conveyed to us by the Holy Spirit. I'm not suggesting that victory will be automatic; it never is. Victory is a process that begins with meditating on Christ and believing that we can conquer defeat.

Breaking that Sinful Habit

We are all born with a powerful sin nature that carries us along like a cork on a river. The more sensitive we are in our relationship with God, the more excruciating our struggle with the sin nature becomes. Paul wrote: "For the flesh sets its desire against the Spirit, and the Spirit against the flesh; for these are in opposition to one another so that you may not do the things that you please" (Gal. 5:17, NASB).

No matter how much we abhor what we see within our lives, self-crucifixion will not bring the slightest relief. Our hope resides in Christ who can change us from the inside out.

Here are some practical suggestions to begin the process.

1. Accept Christ's Lordship in your life as fully as you understand it. Many of us are reluctant, fearing the consequences of a yielded life. How easy it is to commit ourselves to God even while holding back illicit pleasures we have no intention of forsaking.

Most Christians who never find help for their problems are simply not desperate enough. They want victory, but they are afraid of the radical commitment required. For example, a man plagued with lust wants God to deliver him from this sin, but expects God to leave the rest of his life alone. Such a man will never break his sinful thought patterns.

As believers, Christ is rightfully the Lord of our lives. He is our new Master. But we can refuse to submit to Him. We can choose to be double-minded and hold out on our commitment. Thus we thwart the first step toward spiritual freedom. So ask yourself: Am I serious about accepting Christ's Lordship over every part of my life?

2. Our conscious thoughts must be directed toward our position in Christ. This means saturating our minds with Scripture. Jesus told about a man who had a demon exorcised. The demon went to and fro seeking rest but finding none. Then he discovered that the life of the man he had left was clean and empty. So the wicked spirit got seven other demons more wicked than himself and inhabited the man. His latter state was worse than his former (Matt. 12:43-45).

We cannot break with sin without developing habits

of righteousness to replace the evil. The works of the flesh are crowded out by concentrating on the promises of God directed toward us. This involves meditation and memorization of Scripture.

If you are serious about changing your behavior, find Scripture verses which relate directly to the habits you wish to break: sensuality, coveteousness, pride, gluttony, or anger. Then when these thoughts or desires emerge, reject them in the name of Jesus, quoting the verses you have learned. Within time, your thought patterns will change. Thus the victory Christ purchased will be applied to you personally.

Often it is necessary to replace a sinful habit with a constructive activity that will bring joy into your life instead of guilt. For example, a believer who is addicted to television must choose some other projects to replace his habit. You can enrich your life by reading good books and Christian magazines, or by showing hospitality to a neighbor, or by becoming involved in a hobby. These kinds of activity can be cultivated in place of watching too much television. You can use your own imagination to come up with a number of positive activities to replace any sinful habit.

Many believers ask God for deliverance but never fill their *minds* with the positive content of God's promises, or their *lives* with constructive activities. Insisting on our rights as God's children is not an initial act, accomplished once for all. It is a daily process that pushes us irresistibly into a closer walk with Him. The Scriptures do not tell us to break sinful habits without replacing them. "But I say, walk by the Spirit, and you will not carry out the desire of the flesh" (Gal. 5:16, NASB).

3. Thank God for temptation. We will never reach the point where we are no longer tempted. Temptation

will always come knocking on our doors, whether invited or not. God allows temptation (though He does not cause us to sin) to test our loyalty to Him. We cannot say that we love God until we have had to make some hard choices. What shall we choose—the pleasures of sin or the pleasures at God's right hand? The circumstances of life give us ample opportunity to test our allegiance. That's why James wrote, "Consider it all joy, my brethren, when you encounter various trials, knowing that the testing of your faith produces endurance. And let endurance have its perfect result, that you may be perfect and complete, lacking in nothing" (James 1:2-4, NASB). Every trial is an opportunity to develop Christlike responses to the situations of life.

That's why your sinful habit can become a stepping-stone, instead of a stumbling block. God can use it to demonstrate His power in your life. The same strength that made Jesus Christ victorious is available in the person of the Holy Spirit who indwells us. This is possible because you as a believer are "in Christ," identified with the risen Lord and sustained by the greatest power in the universe.

9

You Are Victorious
Over Satan: Authority

Among our rights as believers, one has remained a closely guarded secret. Most Christians know something about the filling of the Spirit, the benefits of prayer and our status as sons of God. But few have any firsthand acquaintance with the one truth that is anathema to Satan and his kingdom of wicked spirits. I speak of our authority as believers.

Perhaps you have experienced times of intense spiritual struggle. Maybe you were filled with anxiety, even though you could not pinpoint specifically what bothered you. Or you may be a slave to pornography, have an uncontrollable temper or find it impossible to witness. Perhaps you suffer from deep depression and emotional conflict. You can be quite sure that Satan is exploiting your weakness. He enjoys using sin—particularly a besetting sin—as his springboard for activity.

Christians who have been involved in the occult have even more intense struggles. They may be subject to moods of depression, strange fears and have their minds bombarded by heinous thoughts. Some hear voices telling them to commit suicide or even to deny Jesus Christ.

What should Christians do in such situations? Simply praying to God for help is often not enough. I've known some believers who have not been delivered even after much prayer and a determination to "get through" to God. Often such praying is done in unbelief. Or, at other times people do not want to face their sin squarely, hence the satanic activity continues.

How can we be sure whether a particular problem is indeed demonic? In the Book of Galatians Paul listed the works of the flesh, which cover a wide gamut of human sins (Gal. 5:19-21). Yet extreme cases of demonic affliction can be discerned quite easily: a compulsive desire to curse Christ, suicidal or murderous thoughts, violent anger or certain physical symptoms (Mark 5:1-10). Often in such extreme cases, the demons must be confronted directly and exorcised. Further scriptural teaching on this can be found in the helpful book, *The Adversary*, by Mark Bubeck (Moody Press, 1975).

My purpose is not to deal with extreme cases, but to consider Satan's work in the life of the average believer. Usually he works under cover, harassing us by exploiting our weaknesses. Unconfessed sin, or sin we have come to tolerate, gives him a basis for his activity.

It follows that the scriptural method of insulating ourselves from satanic attack is to deal specifically with sin. This must be stressed because some well-meaning Christians believe that exorcism is always needed to be freed from demonic affliction.

The most important defense against demonic attack is righteousness, along with an effective use of the Word of God. Satan always needs some reason to trouble us, some sin that gives him a right to our lives. Once sin is confessed and forsaken, his foothold disintegrates. Of course, he still attacks, but we need not succumb to his enticement.

A woman I counseled suffered from demonic attack. She could not concentrate on reading the Bible, became repeatedly angry and had much depression to the point of suicidal thoughts. There was no doubt that this was satanic. Only when demons were rebuked did she have periods of relief. Even though she knew how to use the Word of God, she was not free from this battle.

Finally one day she admitted to me that she had had an abortion before her marriage. She had never been able to accept God's forgiveness for that sin. She needed instruction on how to accept the sufficiency of the blood of Christ. When she began to reject her feelings and believe that God had forgiven her, the guilt was gone. And so was the satanic activity.

This does not mean that Satan will leave us alone if we have confessed our sins. He will adopt a new tactic, confronting us in a dozen different ways. But when we walk in the light (openly expressing ourselves to God in honest confession), we can exercise our authority as believers. When we identify demonic activity, either in our own situation or in the lives of others, we can boldly confront the hosts of hell.

What Is Authority?

There is a difference between authority and power. The New American Standard Bible makes this distinction in Luke 10:19. Christ told His disciples, "Behold, I have given you authority to tread upon serpents and scorpions, and over all the power of the enemy, and nothing shall injure you." Notice that the disciples were not given power over the power of the enemy, but *authority* over the power of the enemy.

You have watched a policeman walk into the middle of the street with his hand raised. All the traffic stops. He does not have power over them—indeed he wouldn't have the power to physically stop a car. But he does have *authority* over the traffic because of his identification with the police department. He has the entire power of the state behind him when he asks cars to stop, though he personally has no power over them at all.

What if a policeman didn't understand the difference between power and authority? Suppose he believed that he must seek power so that he could stop the traffic by the strength of his own right hand.

Foolish? Yes. But no more so than Christians who ask God for power to overcome Satan. God never gives us power as such, but we can exercise our authority which is ours by inheritance as a believer.

What specifically is authority? It is delegated power. It is the right to exercise control in the kingdom because of one's special relationship to the king. It is one person acting in the name of another.

Receiving Authority

I'll never forget the experience I had counseling a believer who had been in the occult. Over a period of weeks it became obvious that demonic forces had captured her mind. When I spoke to her of the power of the blood of Christ, she almost blacked out; at other times she experienced temporary deafness.

Several weeks later I concluded that the demonic forces would have to be confronted directly. Before this session began I prayed, "Lord, give me authority over these evil forces." Abruptly, I sensed I had grieved the Holy Spirit, for I was praying in unbelief. I was doubting God's Word; I was asking for a privilege that I already had, a right inherited by every child of God.

"Lord," I prayed aloud, "forgive me for my unbelief. Thank You that You have given me authority over wicked spirits; thank You that this is my birthright."

Moments later I read a passage of Scripture to this woman that explained our authority over all the kingdoms of evil. Paul prayed that the spiritual eyes of the believers at Ephesus might be enlightened:

So that you may know what is the hope of His calling, what are the riches of the glory of His inheritance in the saints, and what is the surpassing greatness of His power toward us who believe. These are in accordance with the working of the strength of His might which He brought about in Christ, when He raised Him from the dead and seated Him at His right hand in the heavenly places, far above all rule and authority and power and dominion, and every name that is named, not only in this age, but also in the one to come. And He put all things in subjection under His feet, and gave Him as head over all things to the church, which is His body, the fulness of Him who fills all in all (Eph. 1:18-23, NASB).

I hope you read these verses carefully enough to see that (1) Christ's ascension to heaven placed Him above all rule, authority and power and every name that is named, and (2) that all things are under His feet—there is no power in the universe that operates without Christ's permission. So far so good, but here is the third fact that puts it all together: we are *seated with Christ* in heavenly places. As a believer in Jesus Christ, do you realize what this means? *Satan, along with all of his wicked spirits, all the hosts of darkness, are already— this very moment—under your feet!*

When I pointed this out to this woman, the wicked spirits which troubled her came to the surface and using her vocal cords, blasphemed and threatened me. At first, I was frightened, but when I remembered my position in Christ and on that basis commanded them to be silent, they obeyed. Moments later, on the basis of our authority in Christ, God saw fit to expel these spirits from her. (For further instruction regarding such special cases, I again refer the reader to *The Adversary.*)

The point is that we do have authority over satanic forces. We do not encounter Satan with our own strength. Even Michael the archangel when he disputed with the devil about the body of Moses, did not dare pronounce against him a railing judgment, but said, "The Lord rebuke you" (Jude 9). Thus in actual spiritual combat, the archangel deferred to Satan, and put him in the Lord's hands.

Believers, therefore, deal with demons on the basis of Christ's delegated authority. We need not seek a special gift, agonize for power or pray for an experience that will make us victorious over demonic forces. Perhaps this is why Paul spoke of standing firmly on the territory Christ has already conquered (Eph. 6:14). By His death and ascension, Christ defeated Satan. "When He had disarmed the rulers and authorities, He made a public display of them, having triumphed over them through Him" (Col. 2:15, NASB). Satan has no choice but to retreat when we insist upon our rights as God's children.

Also, we can exercise our authority as priests before

God (1 Peter 2:5). Parents especially ought to intercede as priests on behalf of their children. Some parents may have children who have gone deeply into sin. God honors the bold prayers of parents who exercise their authority over satanic forces. I know of some remarkable answers to prayer when parents have prayed, "O God, in the name of the Lord Jesus Christ and the shed blood of the cross, *we* take back the territory that our child has yielded to evil forces." God honors such confidence in our praying. Demonic forces cringe when Christians exercise their authority and command wicked spirits to stop their activity.

Christ Himself gives us the pattern for combating Satan. Three times He quoted the Old Testament, insisting that His life was under its authority. Note that Satan did not leave immediately, for he resists the truth as long as he dares. But eventually, he left and the angels who were hovering nearby ministered to Christ (Matt. 4:1-11).

That's why we ought to study the Word of God, learning passages for the various temptations of life. If you are controlled by chronic anxiety or fear, you may be fighting more than your sinful human nature. Demonic powers may be exploiting your emotional conflict. Deal with this directly by saying, "Begone Satan, for it is written, 'Be anxious for nothing, but in everything by prayer and supplication with thanksgiving let your requests be made known to God. And the peace of God which surpasses all comprehension shall guard your hearts and your minds in Christ Jesus" (Phil. 4:6-7, NASB).

We ought to know the Word of God well enough to quote verses that speak of coveteousness, pride, anger, worry, discouragement, lust and unbelief—whatever sin may tempt you. These are the works of the flesh, but they are also the channels through which evil spirits do their work. When we confidently resist the devil, he will flee from us (James 4:7).

Becoming Involved

Perhaps you have read the last few pages apprehensively, fearing to become directly involved in spiritual warfare. Many Christians have told me, "I believe that if I leave Satan alone, he'll leave me alone. I don't want to get involved."

Without realizing it, these believers have unwittingly conceded the battle to the enemy. *Satan has them exactly where he wants them*—tucked away on the shelf labeled, "Too frightened to fight." Sometimes I lovingly tell such people, "You don't want to get involved? My friend, you are involved. In fact, you've just made peace with the enemy."

Remember, Satan's most successful weapon is *fear.* He'll make you believe that he will create havoc in your home, or ruin your peace of mind if you take his existence seriously. Don't believe this; Satan is a liar and the father of lies (John 8:44). He will bluff you, pushing you as far as your ignorance will allow.

Our conflict is never easy, but it is rewarding. A young married couple who had to come to grips with the reality of satanic activity in their marriage told me later, "Now that we have experienced the power of Satan, we also appreciate the power of Christ more— we cannot take Christianity for granted again."

We cannot be foolhardy in our approach to spiritual warfare. To be successful in exercising our authority the following guidelines are essential.

First, we must confess our sins and be in complete fellowship with God. As mentioned, evil forces use unconfessed sin, or a sinful habit as a wedge to exploit our weaknesses. To protect ourselves from such attacks, we must learn to keep our accounts with God current. We must stand on the promises of the Word, and wear the armor God has provided (Eph. 6:13-20).

Second, when we exercise our authority we will experience remarkable results. God honors our boldness in confronting the enemy. Demonically induced depression subsides; those plagued with endless spiritual defeat often are delivered from a life of failure. But that's where the danger comes in—the danger of becoming proud because satanic forces are subject to us.

No sin sets us up for a stinging defeat as much as pride. Remember the Israelites at Ai? They had just conquered Jericho; huge walls had collapsed in response to their obedience and faith. Since Ai was smaller than Jericho, they thought they could capture the city easily with 3,000 men. But Israel was soundly defeated (Josh. 7:1-5). Be especially careful after spiritual victory.

Christ reproved the disciples for exulting in their authority, "Nevertheless do not rejoice in this, that the spirits are subject to you, but rejoice that your names are recorded in heaven" (Luke 10:20, NASB).

Finally, we must have patience and endurance in the conflict. God will not always work exactly like we think He should; deliverance and answer to prayer will not come as quickly as we would like. God will work, the enemy will be defeated, but not necessarily according to our schedule.

Remember when the disciples came to Christ, confused because they could not cast out a particular demon? Christ chastised the disciples for their unbelief, but later in private conversation explained that some demons do not come out except by prayer and fasting (Mark 9:29).

Why doesn't God give instantaneous deliverance when we exercise our authority? He uses these trials and battles to teach us necessary lessons. Those who have been involved in the occult often experience long battles before they are completely free. In the process they learn of the tenacious power of sin, and the far-reaching consequences of disobedience. Quick and easy solutions breed thanklessness and carelessness.

We need God moment by moment. The trials of life drive us to the living God who wants to lead us to an intimate relationship with Him. God sometimes allows Satan to test our armor to see whether we have all the pieces. But with our feet firmly planted on God's promises, we are victorious in the conflict.

10

You Are Free
From the Law: Grace

Are we under the law today? Ask the average Christian and he will answer, "No, but . . . well, in a sense we are." Such equivocation is understandable. On the one hand no one wants to put us back under Old Testament regulations, yet on the other hand no sensible Christian wants to assert that we are free to do as we please. Part of the problem also has to do with the meaning of the phrase "under law."

One of the major accomplishments of the Cross is that the Old Testament system of law was completely done away in Christ. This is so clear that it cannot be debated. Paul wrote, "For sin shall not be master over you, for you are not under law, but under grace" (Rom. 6:14, NASB). Contrary to popular opinion, Paul taught that being under the law meant that we are slaves of sin, whereas living under grace meant we would be free from sin. Many legalists today believe the opposite is true. For them grace means license to sin, the law means maintaining high standards.

In Galatians Paul presented his most sustained argument that we are not under the law. Returning to life under the law puts us under its penalties and every detail of its intricate requirements. Little wonder the law was a curse—not because it was contrary to God's will, but because it was powerless to save. It could only condemn. Fortunately, "Christ redeemed us from the curse of the Law, having become a curse for us—for it is written, 'cursed is everyone who hangs on a tree'" (Gal. 3:13, NASB). Paul argued that if we are under the law we are not led by the Spirit. Again, contrary to legalists, Paul taught that freedom from the law does not mean lawlessness but is a precondition to walking in the Spirit.

Yet, some well meaning Bible teachers want to put us back under the law. Usually, the argument runs something like this: all of the Old Testament law was done away except the Ten Commandments. Thus we are not under all of the law, but just some of it.

The law was given to the nation Israel as a unit; it was not neatly divided into ceremonies, ordinances and a moral code. Furthermore, to keep part of the law—just to put ourselves under one commandment—obligates us to keep it all (Gal. 5:3; James 2:10). Like one Bible teacher put it, "The law was not a smorgasbord, where you could pick and choose the parts you wanted to keep."

Fortunately, the Scriptures leave us no doubt about this. Read Paul's contrast between the Old Testament era of law and the New Testament age of the Spirit: "But if the ministry of death in letters engraved on stones came with glory so that the sons of Israel could not look intently at the face of Moses because of the glory of his face, fading as it was, how shall the ministry of the Spirit fail to be even more with glory?" (2 Cor. 3:7-8, NASB) The ministry of the Spirit has replaced the law—yes, even the Ten Commandments are a ministry of condemnation. Let us not be afraid to proclaim that we are not under the law today.

The Law Fulfilled

Why did God abolish the law? Its standards reflected His righteousness, but the law as a system was replaced because it was powerless. It could not bring us what we desperately need—righteousness.

To illustrate: a man is drowning. When he comes up for air you read him the law, Code A, Section 12, which reads, "Swimming is prohibited in this area after 6:00 P.M." You might manage to make him feel guilty, but that's all. The law cannot save him from drowning.

The law is always external, demanding, and powerless. "For if the law had been given which was able to impart life, then righteousness would indeed have been based on the law (Gal. 3:21, NASB). If the law could have saved us, Christ's death would have been unnecessary. But the law cannot produce righteousness.

Not only is the law unable to save us, but the law cannot contribute toward our sanctification. We've already quoted Paul's words, that freedom from the law is a *prerequisite* to freedom from sin and walking in the Spirit (Rom. 6:14; Gal. 5:18). To return to the law is to fall back into spiritual bondage; it is to go backward, not forward. The law cannot produce what God desires to see within us. For that, grace must do its work.

How did Christ abolish the law? By fulfilling all of its demands for us. He became a curse for us, absorbing all of its penalties in His own person. Now God declares us righteous because our sin was imputed to

Christ, and His righteousness was imputed to us. Let us say it boldly: we do not owe God the slightest amount of righteousness. His strongest demands were met at the cross. We can shout with gratitude that Christ has "cancelled out the certificate of debt consisting of decrees against us and which was hostile to us; and He has taken it out of the way, having nailed it to the cross" (Col. 2:14, NASB). Thank God, the law can no longer condemn us.

Satan is pleased when believers slip back into law. Putting ourselves under its jurisdiction, he can rightly argue that we sinners deserve to be judged and doomed forever. Now that we are saved, he will try to get us to believe that sanctification comes by the law—obedience to external regulations. If so, we become like the Galatians who began in the Spirit but sought personal perfection by the flesh (Gal. 3:3).

Through Christ, God has made a new arrangement for our Christian life. John explained it, "For the law was given through Moses; grace and truth were realized through Jesus Christ" (John 1:17, NASB).

Needless to say the Israelites in the Old Testament were not saved by the law either, for their sin was ultimately credited to Christ's account (Rom. 3:25). But they were under the law as a rule of life. The law was to govern their conduct; it became the basis for their personal and corporate responsibilities. Disobedience was to be severely punished; obedience was a condition of blessing. God judged them by how closely they lived up to the detailed moral code they were given.

Today we are not under the law; it is not the basis for personal blessing. Nor are we under its penalties. Let us accept this without reservation; if not, we will not appreciate the radical dimensions of God's grace.

But before we discuss life under grace, we must pause to consider a word that has often been misunderstood. Frequently, we hear, "Mr. Jones is a legalist, he's so disciplined, and he'd never do a thing wrong!" Is this legalism? Is obedience to law always legalism? If not, why not? What is legalism, anyway?

The Meaning of Legalism

When we expose the errors of legalism, we must know precisely what we are condemning. A disciplined believer who sets standards for himself, is not necessarily legalistic. Nor is the person who seeks to be obedient to the New Testament commands. He may be, but not necessarily.

Legalism is a *wrong use* of laws or rules. Several different types of legalism are mentioned in the Scriptures and still exist today. First, there are those who believe that salvation can be attained by keeping the law. The rich young ruler wrongly thought that he had kept the commandments from his youth. He thought that would be sufficient for eternal life.

He was wrong. So are many others who think that God will accept them for doing their best. "What else can God expect?" they ask. Of course, God expects infinitely more—so much more that Christ alone meets His requirements.

Second, there is the legalism of the Jews mentioned in the Book of Galatians. They understood that salvation is a free gift, but they believed that sanctification comes by obedience to external rules. They began in the Spirit, but hoped to be made mature in the flesh.

Today their number is legion. Many Christians believe they are spiritual because they do not go to movies, drink, dance or otherwise participate in worldly activities. I'm not suggesting that we do these things, but it is deceiving to think that we are thereby made pleasing to God. If such rules could sanctify us, then even an athiest could be sanctified.

Such rules—which usually vary from church to church and state to state—are of value for keeping us from certain outward sins. But, they cannot help us become Christlike. Sanctification comes from a supernatural change within us, not from abstaining from certain amusements, commendable as this may be.

Finally, there is the legalism of the Pharisees. They not only tried to keep the law for personal salvation, but they also added to the teachings of the Old Testament. All sorts of hair-splitting distinctions were made, hence the Word of God was nullified through their traditions (Mark 7:6-13).

The parallels that exist today scarcely need comment. Often the teaching of the Bible has been so closely related to cultural practices that the standards of a culture have been given equal status with biblical principles. Dress codes, forms of worship, and types of amusements often are identified with spirituality, even when no particular biblical principle is at stake. Christ taught that the outward was not as important as the inward (Mark 7:18-23).

Legalism has two primary characteristics. First, legalists believe that our relationship with God is based on our works rather than on what Christ has already done. Man can only please God by fulfilling the demands of a given law. Second, legalists emphasize outward conduct rather than inward thoughts and motivations. In a word, legalism is *self-righteousness*. It is the belief that God is satisfied with our attempts to obey a moral code.

What value does the law have? It points out sin. Paul wrote, "Therefore, the law has become our tutor to lead us to Christ, that we may be justified by faith" (Gal. 3:24, NASB). The law reflects God's holiness; it is a plumbline that shows us that we are crooked. Paul said that he would not have realized that coveting was sin, except that the law said, "You shall not covet" (Rom. 7:7, NASB). God's standard, regardless of where it is found in the Bible, can be used as a backdrop for explaining the need for God's grace. But to use the law either as a means of salvation or sanctification is to return to what Paul called the "weak and worthless elemental things" (Gal. 4:9, NASB).

Living Under Grace

If we are free from the law, what then is God's standard for us?

Some erroneously think that freedom from the law means that God has relaxed His standard, therefore we can do as we please. That's why Paul warned, "For you were called to freedom, brethren; only do not turn your freedom into an opportunity for the flesh, but through love serve one another" (Gal. 5:13, NASB). Jude warned about those who turned the grace of our God into licentiousness (v. 4).

However, the doctrine of grace does not encourage believers to sin. Grace teaches us not to sin (Titus 2:11-13). Paul was accused of teaching that living under grace breeds lawlessness. His critics said, "Let us do evil that good may come." Paul dismissed the charge and wrote "their condemnation is just" (Rom. 3:8, NASB).

What does it mean to live under grace? Our relationship with God is on an entirely different level. First, we are motivated by our love and thankfulness. The emphasis of the Mosaic law was "obey and you will be blessed." But Christ has already blessed us with all spiritual blessings (Eph. 1:3). He has made us sons, given us the Holy Spirit and promoted us to be heirs with Himself. All of this was freely done without any strings attached.

Since the demands of the law have been met, our motivation is not fear, but love. Paul urged us by the *mercies* of God to present our bodies as living sacrifices, acceptable to God (Rom. 12:1). Why do we love God? To gain His approval? No, for we already have His approval in Christ. John wrote, "We love Him, because He first loved us" (1 John 4:19).

This puts our obedience in a different perspective. For example, every state has laws regarding child abuse. Parents who neglect their children are lawbreakers and can be arrested. But this is not why my wife and I take care of our children. Fear of the law does not get us up at 2 A.M. to comfort a crying child. Because our children belong to us and we love them, we take care of them.

Believers who are motivated by legalism are always anxious to know what is expected of them. They want to do only what is necessary to make themselves look respectable. They crave specific rules so they can know precisely how to behave. They plod along hoping that someday their efforts will pay off. According to the New Testament such people are legalists; they are using the law to establish their righteousness.

A legalistic athlete dislikes football but plays the game to please the coach or avoid other responsibilities. He wants to know exactly what the requirements are, so that he won't attend more practices than necessary. Another athlete plays football for the sheer love of the game. He goes beyond what is expected. He doesn't ask how much he can get by with and still be accepted by the coach. His heart is in the game.

Think of the difference this makes when giving money to God's work. He doesn't want us to give grudgingly or of necessity. To serve God out of a sense of duty is to misunderstand His love and devalue His grace. The incentive of the law used by some evangelical fund raisers is, "If you don't give one-tenth of your income, God won't bless you." The incentive of grace taught in the New Testament is, "For you know the grace of our Lord Jesus Christ, that though He was rich, yet for your sake He became poor, that you through His poverty might become rich" (2 Cor. 8:9, NASB). We give to Him because He gave to us. God is not gratified by our sense of obligation, but joy. He loves a cheerful giver (2 Cor. 9:7).

Second, under grace, God can accomplish what the law could not—change us from the inside out. The process of conforming us to Christ's image cannot be done by a moral code. Christ's definition of sin penetrates far deeper than a list of sins on a church membership card. Adultery is not merely an act, it is first a thought; the same goes for murder (Matt. 5:21-28).

This leads us to a third consideration. Under grace, supernatural power is readily available. In the Old Testament the ministry of the Holy Spirit was restricted; not all believers were indwelt by the Holy Spirit. But since the Day of Pentecost, all believers are temples of the Holy Spirit. Christ's character can now be formed in each of us. We can live supernaturally in a world that is convinced that the supernatural is a relic of past imaginations.

In the Book of Galatians, Paul listed the nine fruit of the Spirit, then added, "Against such things there is no law" (5:23, NASB). There can be no law prohibiting such qualities; but there is no law that can produce them either.

What would happen if we actually did seek the kingdom of God and His righteousness? What if we did set our affections on things above and not on things of the earth? Such obedience is revolutionary to someone who does nothing more than live up to a list of rules. There would be a supernatural aspect to our lives defying human explanation. And perhaps we would understand what Christ meant when He said that He came to give us abundant *life*.

Free from the law? Yes! Free to serve God without guilt, anxiety or hopelessness. Free to respond fully to His generosity displayed in Jesus Christ.

11

You Have Citizenship
in Heaven: Glorification

Two children were counting their pennies. "I have
five!" exclaimed one little girl. "I have ten," replied the
other. "No, you don't!" insisted the first. "You only
have five pennies, too." The second girl was not caught
off guard, "Yes, I only have five pennies here, but my
father promised me five more when he gets home. That
means I have 10."

Counting her chickens before they hatch? Perhaps.
But if she has a trustworthy father, she can confidently
assert that she has 10 pennies, even when 5 of them are
still in her father's pocket.

So it is with believers. Moses left the treasures of
Egypt and chose a life of suffering with his people. A
foolish decision by all counts, except that he stedfastly
believed in Him who is unseen (Heb. 11:27). So confident was Moses of his future rewards, he could refuse
the present rewards without feeling cheated. In his

mind, he had 10 pennies even when his pockets were empty.

The Apostle Paul became so excited about our future that he spoke of it as the present. As long as we are in our earthly bodies we are not yet glorified, but Paul spoke as if God has already completed His work of glorification in us. "For whom He foreknew, He also predestinated to become conformed to the image of His Son, that He might be the firstborn among many brethren; and whom He predestined, these He also called; and whom He called, these He also justified; and whom He justified, these He also glorified" (Rom. 8:29-30, NASB). The word *glorified* is in the past tense, indicating the certainty of its accomplishment. Our glorification is presented as already completed.

Look at this passage again. Verse 29 speaks of God's eternal purpose, those whom He foreknew (foreloved), He predestined to become conformed to the image of His Son. Then verse 30 introduces us to three acts of God that bring His eternal counsel to completion. These are calling, justification and glorification. There is progression in Paul's thought: God calls us, justifies us and then glorifies us. Notice that there is an unbreakable bond between these three actions. In fact, all five of God's works listed here form a continuous chain. Those whom God foreknows and predestinates to be conformed to His Son are *the same* who are called, justified and glorified.

Of this we can be certain: every believer will be glorified, none will be lost. Glorification is so certain that Paul spoke as if it has already been accomplished. Christ has taken the sting out of the experience of death. Now it is a gateway to ultimate personal fulfillment. Glorification is the goal to which God's purpose relentlessly moves.

Anxious to Die

By all standards, death is the most dreaded event. Our society will pay any price to prolong life. Just one more month, or even another day. Perhaps our desire to postpone death reflects our dissatisfaction with God's ultimate purpose. Remember, His work isn't finished until we are glorified. Most of us would like to see God's work remain half finished. We're glad we are called and justified, but we're not too excited about being glorified.

How different was the attitude of Paul. He could hardly wait to die, preferring to be with Christ, which is far better (Phil. 1:23). Only the possibility of helping his brethren in the flesh made him content with this present life. He was constantly looking away to the glory that is to be revealed in us.

A pastor told me of his conversations with a Christian woman dying of cancer. He asked her if she wanted prayer for healing. "Oh, no," she replied, "I've lived a fairly long life. I've talked this over with the Lord—my time has come to see Him." Unfortunately, her children didn't share their mother's perspective. They tried to postpone her entrance into heaven with more tests, chemotherapy and advanced technology.

"Please tell my children to stop interfering with God's plan for my life," she told the pastor. With the help of the treatments she lived one month longer, then died. Here was a woman itching for glorification, anxious for the Lord to complete the work He had begun in her life.

Lest I be misunderstood, let me add that I am in sympathy with the medical profession and rejoice in the advances made to fight disease. I would be the first to submit myself to any such treatment if I were ill. My point lies in another direction: how differently we would view death if we considered it as an opportunity for God to finish what He has begun. Calling and justification lead to glorification, either now or in the near future. If we could postpone our deaths forever, we would not be doing ourselves a favor. We'd only be robbing ourselves of our coronation day.

Today scientists are investigating whether there is life after death. People who are presumed dead and then return to life tell stories about seeing light, feeling great peace or even meeting Jesus Christ. They report that death need not be feared since there is no judgment.

How foolish! Of course, these reports may be true. All this and more can be attributed to an angel—the angel of light whose delight is in deluding the unsaved into preferring their own visions to the authority of Christ. We can be grateful that modern man has awakened to the realization that death doesn't end it all. But unfortunately this awakening has brought deception. Human beings simply do not have the credentials to speak about death (or life after life) with authority nor to interpret such experiences.

Jesus Christ alone is qualified to guide us into the vast unknown. Since He is the only One who has returned from the grave, He tells us accurately about life after death. We are not dependent upon the reports of those who have stood at the threshold of death and returned to tell about their fleeting visions.

Life in Glory

Ever wonder what it will be like to live in heaven? It's hard to visualize, but of this we are certain: it will be much better than we can imagine. Paul wrote, "Things which eye has not seen and ear has not heard, and which have not entered the heart of man, all that God has prepared for those who love Him" (1 Cor. 2:9, NASB).

First, we shall have new bodies. The Scriptures attribute dignity to the human body. Plato, a Greek philosopher, made a sharp distinction between the soul and the body. He taught that all sensible objects were not only imperfect, but of relatively little value. The body was considered as a prison which confines the soul. The soul would be better off if it were free from this excess baggage.

Today, many Christians still accept his teachings. Recently, I read a book on death written by an evangelical who looked upon the body as the prison of the soul. Not surprisingly, he recommended that when a believer dies, his body should be cremated within twenty-four hours, and *then* a memorial service be held in honor of the dead one, without the body present. He deplored the idea of preparing a body for burial and having relatives mourn over it.

Although his view sounds logical, it is not scriptural. The body is not a vile thing, a prison of the soul. Even though it will decay and return to dust, God considers this dust to be of such value that He will resurrect it in the last day. Admittedly, the resurrection body will be remade and its essence will be different from the material substance we know. But it is this material substance, this earthly body, that God will transform (1 Cor. 15:42-44, 52-53). We have reason to believe that the resurrection body will not be created ex-nihilo. It will be the earthly body radically changed into a spiritual body.

Consider Christ. If His resurrection body had not been in some way a metamorphosis of His earthly body, then His body could have remained in the tomb when He appeared to His disciples. Significantly, the tomb was empty because the corruptible body had put on incorruption, the mortal had put on immortality. His wounds show the continuity of His risen body with His crucified body. He even ate food, yet He appeared in a room without opening the door. He ascended into heaven in a cloud.

Scripturally, the body is an integral part of the total self. A person is a material and spiritual unity. Any future destiny of man must include the destiny of the whole person—body, soul and spirit. In heaven we shall be the same people we were on earth—the same body, soul and spirit—though all three shall be adapted for a heavenly existence. On the Mount of Transfiguration the disciples conversed with Moses and Elijah—the real Moses and the real Elijah. No replicas, no stand-ins.

We shall recognize one another in heaven since we will know even as we are known (1 Cor. 13:12). Presumably if Peter, James and John recognized Elijah and Moses, we will too. Paul comforted the believers at Thessalonica with the assurance that they would see their loved ones again in the presence of the Lord (1 Thes. 4:13-18).

Death will be abolished. No more backaches, nausea or cancer. Accidents will be impossible. Spatial limitations will give way to a whole new order of existence. "We shall be like Him, because we shall see Him just as He is" (1 John 3:2, NASB).

Second, glorification means that our souls will be perfected. Our goal is to become perfect (mature) in our walk with God. But we will never experience complete perfection until our entrance into heaven. The result of justification is that Christ will present us perfect to the Father. "Now to Him who is able to keep you from stumbling, and to make you stand in the presence of

His glory blameless with great joy" (Jude 24, NASB). What is true of us now legally (our perfection) will become true of us in experience. Our arrival in the New Jerusalem will mark the end of conflict and failure.

In heaven, earthly restrictions will be removed. First, we will be delivered from the deception of sin, for no longer will we face temptations that vie for our commitment. The old nature will be eradicated, and Satan will be confined to the pit. No longer will we have to choose between good and evil. Our only desire will be to do God's will. Second, we shall be free from emotional trauma, for God Himself "shall wipe away every tear from their eyes; and there shall no longer be any death; there shall no longer be any mourning or crying or pain; for the first things have passed away" (Rev. 21:4, NASB).

God shall make every provision for our comfort. The limitations of earth will fade as the old arrangements give way to the new. The cycle of nature will be replaced by the divine presence. There will be no days, months, or years. No demanding schedules, no traffic jams. No weather forecasts. Just eternity in the presence of our Saviour.

Look at John's description: "And I saw no temple in it, for the Lord God, the Almighty, and the Lamb, are its temple. And the city has no need of the sun or of the moon to shine upon it, for the glory of God has illumined it, and its lamp is the Lamb" (Rev. 21:22-23, NASB).

Third, we shall establish new relationships. Our time will not be spent discussing past presidential elections or the last world series. These conversations, though quite proper to earth, will be obsolete in heaven.

The focal point of our new environment will be God Himself. When John was given a glimpse into heaven, he saw a throne and on it sat One whom John does not describe. Language cannot capture the majesty of the Almighty, the Ancient of Days.

All of the activity in heaven rotated around that throne. Above it was a rainbow, before it sat the 24 elders. From the throne proceeded lightnings, thunderings and voices. Before the throne was a sea of glass with seven lamps signifying the presence of the Holy Spirit (Rev. 4).

We, too, shall be preoccupied with the triune God—the Father who chose us, the Son who died for us, and the Holy Spirit who now indwells and empowers us. We will worship and serve our Creator. We shall see His face and His name shall be in our foreheads (Rev. 22:3-4). Eternity cannot exhaust the plans God has prepared for His children. Our eternal fellowship with God, far from becoming routine, will be the ultimate fulfillment of every human aspiration. Then the words of the creed will become reality, "The purpose of man is to know God and enjoy Him forever."

What about our relatives and friends? We will see and know them, too, rejoicing together in the presence of the Lamb. Of course, our earthly family structures will be dissolved. True, we shall know our parents as our parents forever, and our children as children. But there will be no marriages, no nuclear family units. There will be one family with a new Head. To fellowship with the saints of both the Old and New Testaments, along with numerous heroes throughout church history, staggers the imagination.

To Be or Not To Be

Our future glorification ought to remind us of how quickly our earthly life passes. When Paul faced death, he wrote that the time of his departure had come

(2 Tim. 4:6). That word *departure* was often used for the loosening of bonds or fetters. Death for Paul meant that he would be freed from a Roman dungeon to live in the courts of heaven. But the word was also used for loosening the ropes of a tent, or a ship. Paul had made many journeys across the roads of Asia Minor, and had frequently sailed on the Mediterranean Sea. Now he was about to launch out for a new destination, leaving the confines of this earth to arrive in heaven.

We are but pilgrims and strangers, always homesick for our final destination. Each day the end of the journey is nearer. We cannot become attached to the world, for we must leave it shortly.

Let us learn from the two men who slept in a tent each night as they made a long journey. Said the man to his travel companion, "Don't drive in the stakes too deeply, for we are leaving in the morning."

Perhaps Paul was so excited about heaven because he had had a glimpse of it (2 Cor. 12:4). For a fleeting moment he saw and heard things which could not even be spoken, for they could not be compared to our present surroundings. Paul's confidence in Christ was so firm that he looked forward to death with anticipation.

Paul's attitude contrasts sharply to that of Hamlet. When Hamlet delivers his famous soliloquy, he begins by saying, "To be or not to be, that is the question." His problem is whether to live or to die. If he continues to live, he faces nothing but misery. If he dies, he cannot be sure he will be better off. He adds, "In that sleep of death what dream may come?" Hamlet is backed into a corner. He dreads living and fears death. Whether he lives or dies, he has lost.

Paul proclaimed the opposite. "But I am hard-pressed from both directions, having the desire to depart and be with Christ, for that is very much better" (Phil. 1:23, NASB). Paul, like Hamlet, could not decide whether he wanted to live or die, but for a different reason. For Paul both life and death were acceptable. He would win either way. For him to live was Christ, with all of the resources which that relationship implies. To die was gain, for that would bring Him into the very presence of the Lord he loved. Hamlet said in effect, "Either way, I lose." Paul said, "Either way, I win." Christ made the difference.

Little wonder Paul wrote that we have already been glorified. God will finish what He has begun in us. Though we live on earth we have already established legal residence in heaven. God's promise is so certain we can speak of heaven with the confidence of a permanent resident.

12

How Then Should We Live?

Imagine what it would be like to have our experience catch up with our theology. The gap between what we are in Christ and our performance is often embarrassing. If only it were as easy to *do* the truth as it is to *know* it.

God, in bringing us to Himself, has cleansed, accepted and empowered us. He has taken us into confidence, sharing His intimate thoughts. Even the master-servant relationship is inadequate to express our new relationship with Him. Christ said, "No longer do I call you slaves; for the slave does not know what his master is doing; but I have called you friends, for all things that I have heard from My Father I have made known to you" (John 15:15, NASB). To us God has given blessing upon blessing, privilege upon privilege.

But how do we embrace these promises? How do we translate our position in the heavenlies into practice?

Shifting Our Focus

To begin, we must welcome every conflict as an opportunity to shift our focus to God. We short-circuit opportunities for spiritual growth when we consider every problem as a setback rather than a stepping-stone. God intended that the harsh realities of life, complete with powerful temptations and suffering, act as an alarm system to push us closer to Himself. If you are submerged in personal conflict, you can be sure that God is calling. Blessed are those who see the hand of God in the haphazard, inexplicable and seemingly senseless circumstances of life.

For this reason the Christian life is never easy. Being a Christian does not exempt you from the universal trials of life. John Bunyan in *Pilgrim's Progress* correctly described the way to the celestial city as beset with temptations, discouragements and satanic warfare. Even when the road does not seem hazardous, we are still faced with choosing between God and the world.

That's the way God intended it. If He wanted to make our journey less treacherous, He could have arranged it. He could give us robust health, an exciting vocation and financial success. Then He could exterminate the devil so that our spiritual commitment would encounter less resistance. Victory, the kind the Apostle Paul spoke about, would be more easily within our grasp. Our lives would be a credit to our Father in heaven. And there would be fewer casualties en route to the celestial city.

But God has planned otherwise. The struggles of life are designed to conform us to the image of Christ. We need many clear-cut occasions to choose between God and our carnal desires. God is not primarily concerned about alleviating suffering, though He sometimes graciously does so. Nor does He shield us from temptation, though He does promise a way of escape (1 Cor. 10:13). Obviously, He does not exist to make our lives easier. In fact, sometimes He makes life harder in order to test our allegiance to Him. That's why James wrote, "Consider it all joy, my brethren, when you encounter various trials" (1:2, NASB).

Is your problem worry? Anger? Sensuality? Pride? Gossiping? Gluttony? You will never overcome such vices unless you look at them as opportunities—pressure points at which God's strength can be proven. More is at stake than your personal victory. Conflict is the main ingredient in God's character development program.

If you are serious about becoming what God intends you to be, readjust the focus of your attention. Habitually "keep seeking the things above, where Christ is seated at the right hand of God. Set your mind on the things above, not on the things that are on the earth" (Col. 3:1-2, NASB). Remember, the failures of life are one of God's ways of getting our attention, urging us to look for His direction. He wants us to choose how we shall live: by circumstances or by faith.

Living By Faith
The life of faith is not easy, for we are asked to believe that which seems contrary to ordinary experience.

We are confronted by two pictures, one is of us as we are in Christ: sons of God; indwelt by the Holy Spirit; joined to the Son; considered as God's special possession; and assured of our future glorification. Then there is another picture of what some of us are like in the world: pessimistic, guilt-ridden, irritable, touchy, critical, weak and perhaps emotionally unsettled. Faced with such an apparent contradiction we must make a choice. Shall we believe what God has said or shall we follow the path of least resistance and give in to our feelings? It boils down to this: which portrait shall we live by?

One danger in the Christian life is that we base conclusions on human observation. We have a hunch that God no longer cares about us because of what He has allowed in our lives. We feel that He no longer accepts us because we have sinned, and so *ad infinitum.* We let our circumstances and feelings dictate our theology.

The Israelites exemplify this. Whenever they were hungry, thirsty or threatened by a greater power, they initiated a theological discussion. The topic: Is God with us or not? Their concept of God and their attitude toward His promises were based on the situation at hand.

Clearly we face a dilemma. Our emotions, inclinations and circumstances point in one direction, while God's description of us points in another. We cannot live by both, for they cancel each other. Faith means that we must not merely believe what God has said, but we must also *disbelieve* what our experiences seem to tell us.

Can our inclinations and observations actually be wrong? If I see myself as unloved, unacceptable to God, and powerless, might I be mistaken? Yes!

Left to our private observations we would conclude that the sun revolves around the earth. What could be more obvious than the fact that the earth is stationary and the sun moves from the east to the west? Yet that conclusion is dead wrong. Astronomers have told us that the sun never rises; rather, the earth turns, tilting on its axis toward the sun. Our common sense conclusions can be misleading sometimes.

So it is with our interpretation of the events of life. Hunches and feelings are not a reliable guide to understanding the real you; God's statements invalidate our distorted self-image. If He says He loves us—and He does so repeatedly—then we *are* loved whether we feel like it or not. If we have been seated in heavenly places, then we are in God's presence even when He seems distant. In Christ, our acceptance before God is complete and secure, even when we are disappointed in ourselves.

Let's suppose you are facing a situation in which it seems that God is *not* at work. Maybe you are plagued with guilt; perhaps you are experiencing emotional trauma, sickness or have just been laid off your job. God seems far away. How does He want us to respond to such an experience?

Henry Teichrob in his seminar on *Christian Reality* explains it clearly: "In practical terms the Lord Jesus is seen in the life of the believer by the responses made to life situations. The Christian who responds in negative ways with anger, malice, vengeance, criticism, envy, fear, discouragement, despair and depression is simply not yielding his life to the Spirit of God. His responses arise out of his determination to have things his own way. Each negative response is a demonstration of his self-centeredness. He reacts as if God is making a mistake in allowing testing circumstances to arise in his life. Essentially these responses are expressions of rebellion and are the works of the flesh."

On the other hand, Teichrob continues, "The glory of the Lord is always revealed in His own when the responses to life situations are *positive*. Accepting our circumstances with tranquility, faith, love and hope reveals Christ. Faith knows that our Lord is in charge and He wants to take our lives and demonstrate His power. *It is not the circumstances of life which determine our destiny—it is our reactions to them.*"

How tragic that so many Christians seek victory in terms of "feeling just right." If we have confessed our sins, we can thank God for forgiveness whether we feel forgiven or not. If we have committed our lives to the Lord, we can thank Him for being in charge even when it appears that everything is going wrong.

Henry Teichrob concludes, "God does not allow us to find a life of victory on physical, chemical or psychological terms. It is found by faith and faith alone. Faith often runs counter to feeling. Even the attempt to find victory in feelings is a sin in the life of the believer. It is simply 'walking in the flesh.' We must repent of the sin of assessing the reality of the Christ-life on the basis of feeling." In short, we walk by faith, not sight (2 Cor. 5:7).

A few years ago an airplane crashed into the top of a mountain. The reason? Prior to the crash the pilot realized that his instrument panel had gone askew. The plane's equipment indicated he was flying off course, and headed for disaster. But the pilot knew better. His intuitive sense of direction told him that the instruments were wrong, and his own judgment of the terrain beneath was reliable. Within an hour he crashed.

The irony was that his judgment was *not* correct. The mechanical instruments were accurate. If he had followed their readings and rejected his own intuition, the crash would not have occurred.

God wants us to fly with His equipment—the Word of God. As the Creator He can tell us who we really are. He knows our needs, and has painstakingly spelled out the remedy. The Bible is our only reliable guide.

Concentrating on who God says we are helps close the gap between our experience and our theology. Meticulous attention to His map will help us avoid that big crash.

Changing Our Thought Patterns

Specifically, now, how do you get *God's* perspective on your life? How can you be changed into the person God says you already are? It is by replacing your wrong thought patterns with God's viewpoint. The furniture of your mind must be replaced piece by piece.

A man recently released from prison was having difficulty adjusting to his freedom. He tried this experiment: he took a glass bottle with a distinct shape and crammed it full of wires, some small, some large. After several days he then smashed the bottle with a hammer. The result? The majority of the wires did not jump back to their original position, but retained the shape of the bottle. Those wires had to be straightened out one by one.

The man had made his point: it is possible to be free and still retain the traits of bondage. Even after a man is liberated he must adjust to his freedom and carefully dismantle the habits of the past.

All believers are legally free in Christ, but we can still be enslaved by the fantasies of the flesh and the vices of the world. We can yield, surrender and "pray through," but our minds will revert back to familiar territory the moment our experience wears thin.

The first step in cleaning our minds is to identify specifically the warped perspective of life we have absorbed from the world. We must diagnose our false values and sinful habits. Once the specific problem is identified, God can replace it with the fruit of the Spirit.

Suppose you are a worrier. That sin robs you of joy, peace and faith. Worry is based on a false premise, namely, that we are responsible for what will or will not happen in our lives. Memorize Philippians 4:6 and 1 Peter 5:7, and soak your mind with huge sections of Scripture. Slowly your perspective on life will change and you will begin to experience the peace of God which is the birthright of every true believer in Christ (John 14:27).

Rather than memorize verses at random, take your list of troublesome thought patterns and find verses of Scripture that speak directly to them. Here are some examples: Lust—Phil. 4:8, Col. 3:5; Pride—Gal. 6:14, James 4:6-7, 1 Peter 5:5-6; Bitterness—Eph. 4:31-32, Heb. 12:15; and Gluttony—Rom. 13:13-14, Phil. 3:19.

Memorize these verses so that you have them at your fingertips during the day. (An alternative to memorizing verses is to type them out on small cards so that you have them for immediate reference.) These are the passages that God will use to demolish the present strongholds of your mind and construct a new edifice. These verses can be used in the following ways:

1. Prepare your mind *before* the temptation comes. Let's suppose your boss habitually irritates you. An hour after you arrive at work you wish you could scream. Don't wait until your boss shouts at you before you decide how you will respond—if so, you'll probably react in anger. Use the Word of God in anticipation of what you can expect to happen that day. During your time alone with God, recite the verses you have memorized and claim Christ's victory *before* your boss blows his fuse.

2. Learn to obey the first promptings of the Holy Spirit. If you are tempted to let your mind enjoy a sensual fantasy, deal with those thoughts *immediately.* All of us know when we let our minds skip across that invisible line into forbidden territory. The moment we do so we sense that we are violating the purity that the Holy Spirit desires. That is the moment to say, "I reject these thoughts in the name of the Lord Jesus," and then quote the passages of Scripture you have learned. Un-

doubtedly, you will often fail, but within time your sensitivity to the Holy Spirit will develop.

3. Use temptation as an alarm system—a signal to give praise to God. Suppose that you live with the fear that you might have cancer. Every time this fear comes, stop yourself short and give praise to God. Quote Romans 8:35-39 or read a psalm (e.g. 103, 144, 145). Then thank God for all the blessings you have in Christ. Thank Him for forgiveness, for His sovereignty, power, and love. In this way your stumbling block will be changed into a stepping-stone. You'll be praising God rather than pitying yourself.

Following a specific program such as this will give God an opportunity to change your character and to fill your life with the fruit of the Spirit. You'll be learning to adopt His perspective, using His method to become what you ought to be.

Reflecting God's Image

Remember Moses on Mount Sinai? He was in the presence of God and his face shone. But he did not know that he was aglow with God. While others could see the transformation, he didn't know that he bore the reflection of God.

Paul said that is what God wants to do with us. "But we all, with unveiled face beholding as in a mirror the glory of the Lord, are being transformed into the same image from glory to glory, just as from the Lord, the Spirit" (2 Cor. 3:18, NASB). The process begins at our conversion and ends with our glorification. En route, God has given us everything needed for the journey. He has adopted us into His family and promised us limitless resources.

Day by day we can experience a transformation, which others usually perceive. Gradually we become what God says we already are in Jesus Christ. He is waiting for us to believe that He is as good as His Word.